Needs

International Library of Philosophy

Editor: Ted Honderich
Professor of Philosophy, University College London

A catalogue of books already published in the
International Library of Philosophy
will be found at the end of this volume

Needs

Garrett Thomson

ROUTLEDGE & KEGAN PAUL

London & New York

First published in 1987 by
Routledge & Kegan Paul Ltd
11 New Fetter Lane, London EC4P 4EE

Published in the USA by
Routledge & Kegan Paul Inc.
in association with Methuen Inc.
29 West 35th Street, New York, NY 10001

Set in Times
by Inforum Ltd, Portsmouth
and printed in Great Britain
by T.J. Press, Padstow, Cornwall

Library of Congress Cataloging in Publication Data

Thomson, Garrett.
Needs.

(International library of philosophy)
Bibliography: p.
Includes index.
1. Need (Philosophy)   2. Desire (Philosophy)
I. Title.   II. Series.
B105.N33T47 1987   128   87—4620

British Library CIP Data also available

ISBN 0–7102–1114–7

For Renata

CONTENTS

ACKNOWLEDGMENTS

I wish to thank Dr James Griffin, Derek Parfit and David Wiggins for their encouragement and patient criticism during the writing of this book. I profited tremendously from discussions with them and their comments led to some fairly extensive revisions, mostly in the direction of clarification.

I am also grateful to Mrs Jean Austin, Dr Raymond Frey, Professor Richard Hare, Steven Lukes and Alan Montefiore for their comments, and to Dr Adrian Moore and his continued help. I read an earlier draft of Chapter III to my former colleagues at Liverpool University; their comments led me to restructure the chapter.

Finally, I am most grateful to my wife, Renata, who gave me time, strength and support. I dedicate this book to her.

INTRODUCTION

The concept of a need is employed frequently at the heart of many types of theories, for example in educational, political, social and moral theories. These diverse uses of 'need' have in common a concern for values and priorities. 'Need' has a tone of seriousness and it appears to provide us with a very direct and simple way of evaluating objectives, aims and ideals in any field of enquiry where it is people that matter. The concept of a need appears to be ideally suited for evaluating any human concern.

It is not clear why 'need' should be tailor-made for this type of role. It would seem that the concept has special features, but until we are better placed to understand these, we are in constant danger of using the concept inappropriately and with confusion, and of using the term 'need' merely as a rhetorical device.

To begin the investigation, we require a rudimentary character-isation of why the concept of a need may be thought to be special. In intuitive terms, I suggest the following:

1 Needs are objective in the sense that it is a discoverable matter of fact what needs people have and this fact has an intrinsic bearing on what we ought to do. 'Need' allows us to pass from an 'is' statement to an 'ought'.
2 Needs are unimpeachable values. We cannot say truly that people ought to have different needs, and hence needs provide a bed-rock for evaluation.
3 Needs are a matter of priority. What we need is something which we cannot do without, and hence is an overriding reason.

These rough claims are supposed to articulate general features of the concept of a need by virtue of which the concept is such a potent and apt instrument for evaluating social policy and individual concerns and ideals. All three claims require explanation, argument, and qualification.

My primary aim is to explain the ways in which the concept of a need functions, and an important part of this must be to reveal its distinctive empirical content and show how that content relates to its evaluative role. This requires an elucidation of other concepts. For example, to characterise a fundamental need we must elucidate the notion of harm. In so doing, I contrast objective non-desire-based theories with subjective desire-based theories of harm and argue that both types of theory are inadequate. In order to find an alternative view of harm, I examine the notion of a desire. Once a desire-based theory of harm has been rejected, we avoid the view that all needs are simply the necessary conditions for the satisfaction of desires. Furthermore, in order to highlight features of 'need', I contrast it with 'desire'.

The major themes of this book can be summarised in the following claims:

1 Not all needs are instrumental; the notion of a fundamental or non-instrumental need is a normative concept because it pertains to serious harm (Chapter I).
2 Fundamental needs are inescapable (Chapter II).
3 Harm should be defined in terms of interests and not desires (Chapters III and IV).
4 Harm is not indefinitely plastic (Chapter V).
5 The concept of a need is in a certain respect vague but this does not mean that needs are relative (Chapter VI).
6 Needs must be distinguished from desires and needs override desires as prudential reasons (Chapter VII).
7 The concept of a need cannot be analysed prescriptively (Chapter VIII).
8 'Need' makes a virtue of necessity (Chapter IX).

An analysis of 'need' not only points forward into social and moral theory, but also affords us a welcome chance to study familiar problems concerning the nature of welfare, value and man from a new angle.

I

CLASSIFICATION AND CLARIFICATION

Need is a very important concept comparatively little studied by philosophers.

Kenny.[1]

I

One day, sit in Parliament and listen to the proceedings. You will be struck by how frequently the word 'need' is used. You may also notice that the term is employed in a variety of ways, often without a clear conception of its meaning.

Anybody thinking about human needs and their significance would have to consider the rhetoric and semantics of the term 'needs'. We can imagine such a person, eager to discover what a need is and how our needs could best be met, quickly becoming entangled by conceptual problems and perhaps turning to analytic philosophy for help or guidance. But help would not be there. Modern philosophers have had surprisingly little to say about 'need' and what has been said is often contradictory. To give examples:

Is 'need' normative?

The term 'need' is mainly normative.   R. Peters
Does A need X? is . . . not a normative question.   A. White

1

Classification and clarification
Does 'need' entail 'lack'?

If a man needs X then he must lack X.   R. Wollheim
It is a mistake to suppose that to need something is to lack it.
      A. White

Are needs drives?

'Needs' suggest . . . striving or motivation. . . .   Springborg
Reference to needs does not explain actions.   Peters[2]

The most central of these disputes is the first, because so much hinges on it. If the verb 'need' were never normative, as claimed by White, then all talk of needs relating to human welfare would be inappropriate, and the contrast between essential needs and luxuries would be bogus. In short, 'need' would be a concept without any intrinsic bearing on values and reasons for action, and consequently would be less interesting and relevant. White says:

> It would be a mistake to suppose that the notion of 'need' can be analysed in terms of a reason.[3]

Against White, I contend that the verb 'need' does have a normative as well as a non-normative meaning. This has important implications.

It is a common view that all needs are instrumental,[4] that one can only need something for a particular purpose or goal. If this is so, all talk of human needs *tout court* is misplaced and all sentences of the form 'A needs X' are elliptical as we must always specify a purpose for which a thing is needed. If we must always specify a relevant purpose or if all needs are instrumental, the concept of a need cannot be of help in trying to assess the worth of our aims and goals. There is no question of some goals and aims meeting our needs better than others, because all needs are themselves relative to an aim or goal. Under analysis, through this sceptical view of 'need', much of the magic of the concept evaporates. However, this sceptical view is based on the belief that the verb 'need' is never normative, which is inadequate semantically.

I shall argue that not all needs are instrumental, and that we are forced to acknowledge this by a proper classification of the usages of 'need', a classification which recognises that the verb can be both normative and non-normative and which explains why the term 'need' should be common to the different usages of 'need'. We require a unified account of the variety of ways in which the term is used. At least in English, the word 'need' occurs grammatically as a full verb, as a modal auxiliary and as a noun. It is also used as an archaic adverb reinforcing 'must' as in 'we needs must die'.[5] We can safely ignore its use as an adverb and treat the verb and the auxiliary together,[6] which leaves the noun and the verb/auxiliary forms. These must be treated separately because not every sentence in which the verb 'need' occurs indicates the existence of a need.[7] By first showing that the verb has a normative as well as a non-normative meaning, I shall argue that not all needs are instrumental.

1 In order to conduct electricity an element needs a free
     electron.
2 To be female one needs an XX chromosome.
3 To meet the Devil one needs to go to hell.
4 To die one's brain needs to stop working.

It is obvious from these examples that the verb 'need' can be non-normative. In each of these sentences the verb only indicates that one state of affairs is a necessary condition for the obtaining of another. It simply indicates a certain relation of necessity and does not recommend. In this sense of the verb, to say that X is needed is to say that X is a necessary condition. Thus the only semantical restriction on the way this use of the verb can occur significantly in sentence is that it pertains to a necessary condition in accordance with the following schema:

A needs X in order for A to ϕ in circumstances C if and only if X is a necessary condition of A's ϕ-ing in circumstances C.

So long as 'need' is used non-normatively there is no logical restriction on the way we complete the schema. This meaning of the term does not fix or determine what the various schematic letters should stand for. Clearly the meaning of 'a necessary condition' does not change however we fill in the scheme 'X is a necessary condition of Y'. The phrase has the same meaning in 'friendship is a necessary condition of the good life' and in 'having a free electron is

3

a necessary condition of an element conducting electricity.' Similarly, 'need' has the same meaning in 1 to 4 as it does in:

5 In order to survive one needs food.
6 In order to flourish one needs friendship.

If 'need' is non-normative in 1 to 4, then it is also non-normative in 5 and 6 (given that it does have the same meaning). This point might mislead us into thinking that the verb 'need' is never normative, but of course it shows no such thing. It only shows that when 'need' is used non-normatively the meaning of the term places no restrictions on the way we fill in the schema. This does not exclude 'need' from having a normative meaning as well. The verb 'need' can be normative. Consider the linguistic evidence. For example, contrast the 'need' statements 1 to 4 with the following unqualified 'need' claims:

7 Britain needs the fresh start of the Alliance.
8 I need your love.
9 This child needs food.

These claims are normatively strong: they recommend the Alliance, love and food as things which it would be disastrous or damaging to lack. Even if the specific content of these claims is still obscure, their practical force is clear and this force is due to the term 'need'. This can be appreciated by substituting in 7 to 9 'desire' or 'want' for 'need': the resultant sentences lack the seriousness of the originals.

The normative claim 'A needs X' implies that X is practically necessary, that is, indispensable or unforgoable. In this sense of the term, what I *need* for myself is something that I just cannot do without, and thus it is a contradiction to say to the boss: 'I *need* a rest but this is no reason for me to have one.' The non-normative verb contains no element of practical necessity. If my wife asks me for my pen and I acquiesce to her demand, it is self-consistent for me to reply: 'Although I need this pen in order to finish my letter, I can do without it.' Even though the notion of practical necessity is quite vague, this much is clear: if X is necessary, indispensable or unforgoable, then the lack of X must be seriously bad or damaging, and consequently there must be very good reasons for having X. This is why the statement 'I need X but it would not be seriously bad for me to lack it' is contradictory when and only when 'need' is normative.

The contrast between the two senses of 'need' is one aspect of an important feature of natural language. This is the existence of what

I can only describe as a metaphorical interplay between natural modals and terms that express strong reasons for action. The language of practical judgments is thoroughly and naturally infested with modal terms. For instance, when we say of an event that it can't happen, this could mean one of two things. It can be taken literally to mean that given the circumstances and the laws of nature the event is a natural impossibility. The phrase 'this can't happen' also functions as a plea, meaning that the occurrence of the event would be very bad and that it should be prevented from happening at almost any cost. Many of the terms we have to express strong practical judgments also function to express natural modality. This is true of the terms 'must', 'essential', 'requirement', and 'necessary'. Whatever the root of this rather puzzling interplay is, its general existence gives us reason to suppose that it should and does function in the specific case of 'need'.

The phrases 'it is necessary that p' and 'p is necessary' both have practical and modal force. Since in using 'need' we employ the notion of necessity, we can suppose that 'need' has this practical force of importance too. This is especially obvious with the unqualified forms 'I need –' and 'you need –'. Why the practical force should be more apparent with these unqualified forms is best explained as follows. The term 'need' focuses attention on the putative importance of its object, just as 'must' does in 'this must happen'. It highlights the putative seriousness of the thing which is said to be needed. This focus, however, may be dispersed by the qualifying phrase 'in order to φ', especially when the phrase occurs before the term 'need'. For instance, compare 'I need the money' with 'To go to the cinema tonight I need that money'. The first sounds urgent, the second does not. Obviously, the qualifier may sometimes highlight the putative importance of the object more adeptly than 'need', in which case the occurrence of the term 'need' in the sentence will appear almost superfluous. For example, take 'In order to prevent the greatest disaster of all time, you need to V'. Not much of the normative impact of this sentence is lost by substituting 'should' or 'ought' for 'need to'. On the other hand, in a sentence like 'you need to V' much of the tone of seriousness is lost by substituting 'ought' or 'should'.

'X is necessary' can be taken in two senses: in the modal sense of being a necessary condition, and in the practical sense of being unforgoable.[8] In using 'need' normatively, we exploit this ambiguity

5

of the term 'necessary'. The normative claim 'A needs X' makes a virtue of this ambiguity by combining both senses of the term 'necessary': the claim is true when X is practically necessary simply because it is a necessary condition of φ. Therefore, it is a mistake to ignore the normative element of practical necessity in 'need' and regard the verb as always non-normative, but we must not err the other way by forgetting the modal element of natural necessity and treating the normative verb as non-modal.[9]

The normative and the non-normative senses of the verb 'need' are related in that the latter is contained as part of the meaning of the former. The normative verb is also modal.

A needs X (normative) if and only if
A needs X (non-normative) in order to φ and φ-ing is vitally important.

When 'A needs X' does recommend X it means more than just that X is a necessary condition, and more than just that X is practically necessary. It means that X is practically necessary because it is a necessary condition of φ. This places a logical constraint on φ. So, whereas the non-normative sense of 'need' does not place any restrictions on what 'A's φ-ing' stands for in instances of the schema 'X is a necessary condition of A's φ-ing in circumstances C', the normative sense of the term does; the restriction being that what is specified by the antecedent 'A's φ-ing'[10] must be a matter of importance. This is the difference between the two senses of 'need': the normative sense is equivalent to the non-normative sense plus the logical restriction that what is specified by the antecedent must be a matter of great importance. The normative use of 'A needs X' entails that what X is necessary for is important and the non-normative use does not.

If this characterisation of the normative sense of 'need' is correct, then there are at least two ways of falsifying a normative 'need' claim. First, one can show that X is not a necessary condition of A's φ-ing, that A's φ-ing can be true without X. A typical counter-response to this challenge is to retreat to the claim that, even if X is not strictly necessary for A's φ-ing, it is necessary for the efficient, safe securing of A's φ-ing. Secondly, one can falsify a normative 'need' claim by showing that A's φ-ing is not of importance.

There are an indefinite number of true 'need' statements, most of which are uninteresting and few of which indicate the existence of a need. For instance, we cannot conclude from the fact that Jupiter needs a minimum momentum to stay in orbit round the sun that Jupiter has needs. More pertinently, it is true that I need a permit to visit Ulan Batur, even if I have no intention of ever going there and have no need of such a permit. 'I need a permit to visit Ulan Batur' simply says that such a permit is necessary for me to go there, whether I have need of such a permit or not. Not every sentence in which the verb 'need' occurs indicates the existence of a need.[11] For this reason the noun 'need' must be treated separately from the verb.

The most obvious way in which a 'need' statement can indicate a need is by implying the existence of an instrumental need. An instrumental need is always relative to some purpose or goal. To say that a person A has an instrumental need for X is to assert that X is necessary for the completion of some goal or aim of A's. The statement 'A needs X in order to φ' will specify an instrumental need if and only if φ is some goal or aim of A's. The shorter 'A needs X', if read instrumentally, must be elliptical and can be completed only by specifying the purpose for which X is necessary.

The concept of an instrumental need is non-normative. 'A has an instrumental need for X' is equivalent to the assertion that X is necessary for some goal of A's and this says nothing about the value of that goal. Suppose I need certain herbs to fall ill. If it is my intention to make myself ill, I have need of the herbs, even though my intention is without rational foundation and serves me no benefit. A person's aims can be harmful to him, and consequently an instrumentally needed object does not have to be good. It may not be bad to lack such an object. So, the object of an instrumental need does not have to be practically necessary and unforgoable, and 'A has an instrumental need for X' does not entail the normative claim 'A *needs* X'.

Since both lack the implication of practical necessity, the non-normative verb 'need' and the concept of an instrumental need are on a par. An instrumental need is the noun counterpart of the non-normative verb. He who contends that all needs are instrumental will be embarrassed by the question 'What is the counterpart of the *normative* verb "need"?' Remembering that the concept of an instrumental need is non-normative, we should ask: 'What is a normative need and, when does the normative claim "A needs X" indicate such a need?' The normative claim 'A needs X' has the general implication that X is practically necessary. The

7

statement: 'The President *needs* to be shot', if taken normatively, implies that we cannot forgo shooting the President on pain of some disastrous result, but it does not tell us about the President's own needs. A normative 'need' claim will inform us of the President's own needs when it tells us what the President himself cannot do without or forgo on pain of some personal disaster. The normative claim 'A has a need for X' implies that X is practically necessary specifically for A, and X is practically necessary for A when he cannot do without it, when his life will be blighted or seriously harmed without it. If a man must suffer serious harm so long as he lacks self-respect, then he has need of self-respect. Such a need is non-instrumental in that it relates to the overall quality of a person's life rather than to a particular goal that he happens to have. This kind of non-instrumental need I call 'a fundamental need'.

The two concepts 'fundamental need' and 'instrumental need' are as different as bread and cheese, the main difference being that the one lacks, whilst the other has, the normative element of practical necessity. Consequently, 'A has a fundamental need for X' entails the normative claim 'A needs X' but 'A has an instrumental need for X' does not, and fundamental needs unlike instrumental needs are the opposite of luxuries, things which by definition one can do without. It follows from this that if I need £200 to buy some new jewellery and say to my friends 'I need to have £200', they can correctly challenge this claim by saying: 'Sure, you need £200 to buy that bracelet, but you don't *need* £200 because you don't *need* the bracelet.' If I respond to this challenge by reaffirming that I need the £200 to buy the bracelet, or by claiming that the bracelet is necessary for some further goal of mine, then I have missed the point.[12] The proper response is to show that I *need* the bracelet, that for some reason I cannot do without it, and that my life will be seriously impaired if I do not have it. To meet this challenge head-on, it is not enough to show that I have an instrumental need, I must show that I have a fundamental need.

Another difference between the two concepts 'instrumental need' and 'fundamental need' is that the former depends on a person's goals and aims whatever these are, but the latter does not. Even if a person does not have as an aim the improvement of his life and the avoidance of serious harm, he will still have the same fundamental needs. A can have a fundamental need for X without having an instrumental need for it, and fundamental needs are not a special type of instrumental need. Because instrumental needs are relative to a person's goals, if 'A needs X' is an instrumental claim, then it must be elliptical until the relevant goal has been specified. On the other hand, the normative fundamental claim 'A needs X' is not elliptical, because the relevant antecedent is already fixed by the meaning of the term 'need'. To say that A has a fundamental need for X is to assert that so long as A is without X he must suffer serious harm. The concept of a fundamental need determines that the antecedent 'A's φ-ing' in the schema

X is a necessary condition of A's φ-ing in C

must stand for 'A's not suffering serious harm'. Because its antecedent is fixed logically, the fundamental claim 'A has a need for X' is not elliptical.

The differences between the two categories of needs are so significant that it would be a mistake to confuse them. We are forced to recognise both categories by the semantics of 'need'. The normative verb 'need' and the concept of a fundamental need are closely related for they share the implication of practical necessity, which the concept of an instrumental need and the non-normative verb both lack. White's semantics for 'need' is incomplete because it totally ignores the element of practical necessity. Some needs are a serious matter. White loses sight of this tone of importance, and this is why he holds that all needs are instrumental and is unable to account for the special links between a need and harm. In effect, he can only tell us half of the story about 'need'. Once we appreciate that 'need' is sometimes a normative verb, we must recognise that some needs are normative, and following this through, we realise that these are non-instrumental.

A fully adequate classification of 'need' usage will include at least the following categories:

1 Purely modal statements, like 'To become a liquid, hydrogen needs to be cooled', which do not indicate the existence of any need.
2 Purely modal statements which indicate an instrumental or a goal-based need, like 'I need a fork to eat my spaghetti.'
3 Normative statements which do not pertain to the subject's own needs; for instance: 'You, as the strongest swimmer here, *need* to risk your life to save X.'

4 Normative statements which do pertain to the subject's own fundamental needs, like 'I *need* to rediscover my self-respect.'

The schema

X is a necessary condition of A's φ-ing in C

depicts the logical shape of all these statements. All uses of 'need' include the non-normative verb as part of their meaning, because they all pertain to necessary conditions. This means that all 'need' categories should be explained in terms of the logical constraints they place on the antecedent 'A's φing' in the schema. For instance, the concept of an instrumental need places the restriction on antecedent 'A's φ-ing' that it must be some aim or goal of A's. The concept of a fundamental need determines that 'A's φing' must stand for 'A's not suffering serious harm'. Explained in this way the various categories of 'need' usage have a unity.

II

We now have a unified account of the various ways in which 'need' is used. We can employ this account to settle some of the questions philosophers have raised about 'need'.

1 Can inanimate things need?

Despite the fact that many writers have argued that inanimate things cannot need, or do so in the metaphorical extension of the term,[13] the answer to this question must be 'yes'. Sentences such as 'Jupiter needs a minimum momentum to stay in orbit around the sun' are not conceptually odd. This is easily explained: the antecedent and consequent of a necessary condition statement do not have to mention a living organism, and hence inanimate objects and events can be the logical subject of a 'need' statement. In these cases, 'need' is being used correctly as a modal verb, and so this does not constitute an anthropomorphic extension of the term.

If 'need' were an intentional verb like 'desire' then it would be plausible to hold that only living things can need. But 'need' is not intentional like 'desire'[14] because the inference pattern

if A needs X and X = Y, then A needs Y

10

is valid for 'need' but not for 'desire'. Superficially, 'A needs X' seems close in sense to 'A desires X', but needing and desiring are not on a par. Desiring can be something we actively do rather like making a decision or a choice.[15] In terms of its logical shape 'need' is not like this even when it is predicated of persons: to say that A needs X is to assert that the lack of X will of necessity do something to A. 'Need' does not indicate a psychological action restricted to agents.

Another reason why it might be mistakenly thought that the verb 'need' must be restricted to living things is the failure to distinguish properly the verb 'need' from *a* need. Not every sentence in which the verb 'need' occurs indicates the existence of a need. Although statements of the form 'A needs X' can have inanimate things as their logical subject, we cannot say that those things have needs. It is anthropomorphic to say of Jupiter that it has needs. Inanimate things can need, but cannot have needs, because they do not have aims and purposes, and because they cannot he harmed. Consequently, they have neither instrumental nor fundamental needs. So the noun use of 'need', unlike the verb use, is restricted to living things that can have aims and purposes and can be harmed.

2 Does 'need' entail 'lack'?

According to the schema

X is a necessary condition of A's ϕing in C

A needs X independently of whether or not he lacks it. Food is necessary for my survival both when I am eating and when I am not, and thus my claim to need food is not logically inconsistent with the fact that I am enjoying a huge meal. An element needs a free electron to conduct electricity even if it already has such an electron. One can need X and not lack it.[16]

Although 'need' does not necessarily entail 'lack', it often strongly implies it. Normative 'need' claims have an accent of importance and this accent is often used to demand as of right. In saying that he needs X, it is often the speaker's intention to draw the listener's attention to a certain state of affairs (like the fact that he will die without water). This intention carries a conversational implicature, namely either that the speaker lacks X or is likely to lose it. If neither of these things were true, there would be little point in saying that one needed X. Which of the two is implied is usually contextually obvious. That implication and not entailment is operative is apparent from the fact that one can cancel the implication without logical inconsistency; 'along with all other human beings I need X calories per day in order to thrive; but unlike the majority of people in the world, I do get that amount' is quite consistent.

However, these points require qualification. Although 'need' can be used in a way that does not entail 'lack', it can also be used in a way that does. For instance, phrases such as 'the needy' and 'those in need' do entail a lack of what is needed, and Voltaire says: 'work keeps us from three great evils: boredom, vice and need'. By 'need' Voltaire means the lack of what we need.[17]

'Need' has two distinct uses. The logically primary use is that explicated with the schema, where 'need' does not entail 'lack'. The secondary use is where to need is to lack what one needs in the primary sense. Those uses of 'need' which do entail 'lack' are to be explained in terms of the use that does not, and this latter use is logically primary.

The distinction between occurrent and dispositional needs is not unique to either of these two uses, and thus cannot be cited to explain the difference between them. To have an occurrent need for water can be either to lack the water one needs, or to need the water without necessarily lacking it. To have a dispositional need for a vitamin can either mean that one does not yet lack the vitamin one needs, or that one does not yet need the vitamin, even if one does not lack it. It is therefore a mistake to suppose that the primary use of 'need' (the use where one may not lack what one needs) indicates a dispositional rather than an occurrent need. Similarly, it would be a mistake to suppose that the secondary use of 'need' (that use where one must lack what one needs) indicates an occurrent rather than a dispositional need. Also when we talk of needs, sometimes we refer to the things we need, e.g. we talk of water as a need, and the difference between the primary and secondary use of 'need' is reflected in this third use of the term. Needs can be the things we need whether we lack them or not, but they can also be the things which we lack and need.

3 Are needs drives?

It appears that there is one use of 'need' which does not accord with what we have said so far about the term. In certain psychological theories 'need' is used to refer either to a drive or to some inner state that initiates a drive.[18] In these theories a drive is a motivational force instigated by a state of disequilibrium or tension set up in an organism because of a lack.[19] This lack may or may not be the lack of something required for the survival or normal functioning of the organism. Canon originally coined the term 'homeostasis' to refer both to the state of disequilibrium and to the tendency of the organism to restore this equilibrium continually. Thereafter it became fashionable to use 'need' to refer to these internal states of discquilibrium which in conjunction with external stimulation cause behaviour. At first this model was used to explain specific phenomena: why, for instance, rats will consistently choose salty foods when deprived of salt. Homeostatic explanation became common currency, and it and the attendant notion of a drive were extended to cover motivation and explanation of behaviour generally.

This vastly ambitious psychological programme suffers from several well-documented inadequacies only some of which are relevant here.[20] To begin with, quite apart from its internal defects as an explanatory model, the theory misuses the term 'need'. A need is not a homeostatic state that initiates a drive. A homeostatic state is necessarily a state of lack, but it is possible not to lack what one needs. Moreover, the lack of things needed for survival or to avoid serious harm will not necessarily cause drives, and not all drives are caused by the lack of things we need. In fact some drives could be caused by things that we need to avoid. For instance, a person can have a drive to consume alcohol when alcohol is something he needs to avoid. So, 'need', on the one hand, and 'what occasions a drive' on the other hand are quite distinct concepts. Similarly, 'need' and 'drive' are distinct. Drive, like desire, is a motivational concept used to explain behaviour or action; need is not. One may be utterly unmotivated to get what one needs and one may be very strongly motivated towards what one needs to avoid. So needs are not drives. Drives primarily explain behaviour; needs primarily justify it: hunger and thirst must be distinguished from the *need* for food and water. The primary role of needs is to indicate what we ought to do in the name of self-interest: needs are justificatory reasons or values rather than explanatory reasons.

This is not to say that a need cannot be used to explain behaviour. If the concept of a need is a value concept then it must be used to explain those actions which are guided by perception of that value. But when needs do explain behaviour they do so quite differently from how drives and homeostatic states are supposed to. A need explains my behaviour by being the object of belief. My now-frequent visits to the chemist are explained by my belief that I need ginseng (to remain youthful) and by my belief that it is only obtainable there.

Needs can be used to explain behaviour in another way. If an organism pursues things it needs and lacks and when belief explanations are inappropriate, the behaviour may be explained physiologically. Some token physical state, which comes about when the organism lacks what it needs, causes that organism to desire or directly pursue what it needs. The connection between the behaviour and the need is contingent on the graces of evolution. Furthermore, in this causal account the introduction of homeostatic see-saws and hydraulic drives is totally redundant.

The confusion between needs and drives is still common.[21] It arises because of the failure to distinguish necessity and necessitation. The notion of necessity inherent in the concept of a need is confused with the element of necessitation or compulsion inherent in the concept of a drive. A drive compels action and is thus supposed to explain action. A need, however, does not drive us to act, and thus is distinct from a drive.

It may seem that the misuses of the term 'need' in drive theories are less interesting than the internal defects of the drive model of action explanation which I have largely ignored. However, I have stressed the misuses of the term 'need' because these are a potential source of great confusion in so-called 'need'-based normative theories in educational and political philosophy.[22] A person has a fundamental need for X if X is a necessary condition of that person's not being seriously harmed. In discovering what a person's needs are, we discover what a person has a good reason to seek. But if instead of investigating a person's needs, we try to determine what his drives are and call these 'needs', then the recommendatory tone of the term 'need' may be completely misplaced. A person's needs have a bearing on how he ought to live, but drives may have no such relevance, and thus to refer to drives as 'needs' is highly misleading.

For example, much of the work done on the normative ramifications of needs for political and educational philosophy is based on Maslow's hierarchy of needs, but Maslow's theory is not about needs at all: it is a theory of drives. Normative implications follow from a theory of needs, but only follow from a theory of drives given the dubious assumption that objects of drives and objects of needs coincide. This is why it is crucial to separate the two concepts.

4 Is 'A needs X' elliptical?

It is tempting to believe that statements of the form 'A needs X' are always elliptical.[23] It is tempting, because all such statements pertain to necessary conditions, and all necessary condition statements must have an antecedent which is left unspecified by sentences of the form 'A needs X'. If A needs X, then there must be something that X is a necessary condition of. However, 'A needs X' is ambiguous, and on one reading is non-elliptical. The claim is non-elliptical when the meaning of the term 'need' fixes logically what X is necessary for. This only happens when 'A needs X' entails 'A has a fundamental need for X', for then the antecedent must be the avoidance of serious harm. Since the antecedent is guaranteed by the meaning of the term 'need', under this reading 'A needs X' is non-elliptical. This does not mean that we can tell when 'A needs X' is used non-elliptically and when it is not. Thus the possibilities of confusion and misunderstanding are treble, if a person says that he needs X without any further qualification or explanation. First, the claim could be intended elliptically or non-elliptically. Secondly, if it is intended elliptically, then there could be confusion as to what the suppressed antecedent could be, if the context does not make that clear. Thirdly, elliptical uses of 'A needs X' could belong to one of three different categories of 'need' usage. These are purely modal uses which do not indicate needs, such as 'the Sunlight needs eight minutes' said during a lecture on the time it takes for messages to reach us from space; purely modal uses which indicate instrumental needs; and normative uses of the term which do not pertain to the subject's own fundamental needs, such as 'You *need* to complete this masterpiece' when it is clear that the need does not relate to the painter's own welfare and is not a need he has.

'A needs X' can be elliptical, but this point is susceptible to misformulation. It should not be said that the claim 'A needs X' is incomplete because the question 'What does A need X for?' requires an answer,[24] for this question and its answer 'A needs X in order to V' have misleading implications. They imply that A has a reason for needing X. To show why this is misleading, compare this question and its answer with the parallel sentence forms for 'desire' (i.e. 'What does A desire X for?' and 'A desires X in order to V'). To say that A desires X in order to V is to draw attention to the fact that A possesses a reason for desiring X. His desire is instrumental, because it is motivated by his belief that X is a means to V-ing. An instrumental desire must be distinguished from a desire for something instrumental. It is possible to have a non-instrumental desire for something instrumental; for example, hunger is a non-instrumental desire, and food is a means to survival. The question 'What does A desire X for?' implies that A's desire is instrumental. Similarly, the parallel question for need implies A's need is instrumental in the sense that A possesses a reason for needing X. However, what is meant by saying that 'A needs X' is elliptical is not that A's need is instrumental, but that what he needs is instrumental or is a means to a purpose. This is why it is misleading to express the logical incompleteness of 'A needs X' in terms of the question 'What does A need X for?' It suggests that A has a reason for needing X. But A may have no such reason; for instance, he may be completely unaware that he needs X. Furthermore, needing is not something that we actively do, and therefore it is not something that we can have reason to do.

III

The aim of this book is to analyse the notion of a fundamental need. Henceforward, all uses of 'need', whether noun or verb, will serve to indicate fundamental needs unless otherwise stated. Fundamental need claims have a tone of seriousness, but this should not be explicated prescriptively in terms of a special imperatival force operator. Having shown the error of ignoring the normative element in 'need', we want to examine a prescriptivist theory of 'need'.

To capture the special importance of needs, we may say: 'what a person needs, he cannot do without'. We must clarify exactly what this intuitive formula tries to articulate. The format of the project will be to show how the concept of a need effects a classification of states of affairs, and how this gathering of facts provides a person with a reason for action, albeit one that can be overridden. The road to explaining 'need' lies through the content of the concept and how that content determines the status of a need as a value or reason for action. Furthermore, I believe that it is theoretically advisable to make this account as informative as possible, and that the temptation to rest content with a characterisation of needs in terms of general value concepts should be resisted. We should not say 'it is bad to lack what one needs' without specifying the special way in which that lack is bad. Otherwise, the distinctive content of the concept will be lost together with the opportunity to cite general criteria for determining what our needs are.

Compared to the view that the claim 'A needs X' simply prescribes X,[25] it is already a step in the right direction to link the concept of a fundamental need to some notion of serious harm. This link can be forged by specifying what type of harm the concept of a need involves, and by giving an empirical analysis of that notion of harm. In this way, we can give truth-conditions for a fundamental need claim. The laying out of truth-conditions is in itself a direct challenge to the prescriptivist analysis of need.

A perceptive opponent of this kind of philosophical project will direct his attention to the concept of serious harm. By applying familiar arguments about the general nature of value concepts, he will aim to show that the notion of harm, and hence the concept of a need, must include a prescriptive element, because any purely empirical analysis of these concepts cannot do justice to their status as action-directing values. In Chapter VIII, I give an unfamiliar and essentially simple counter-argument to this challenge, which will vindicate treating 'need' and 'harm' as both empirical and value concepts without any imperatival force.

There are also some more specific arguments to be directed against a prescriptive analysis of need and harm. First, Hare urges that harm should be understood in terms of our being deprived of what we desire. He also contends that the relevant notion of desire is prescriptive, because when 'I desire X' is an expression of value it entails an imperative.[26] One of the themes of Chapter III is that we should reject desire-based elucidations of harm, and for that reason Hare's analysis can be rejected. Secondly, it is an important aspect of my treatment of 'need' that needs pertain to the natural limits of choice or that we cannot choose what our needs are. This could not be the case if we could freely alter the substantial nature of harm, for instance, by desiring different things. Such freedom of choice, which is implied by prescriptivism, leads to counter-intuitive results about the nature of harm, and contradicts the thesis that needs are inescapable. For these reasons, the concept of a need should not be analysed prescriptively and need-claims should be treated as assertions with truth-value. Furthermore, the concept of a need does not involve a conflation of practical and natural necessity.[27] The concept, as it were, trades on the metaphorical interplay between these two notions, and does not confuse them. The fact that it does not confuse them does not mean that the concept of a need contains two distinct and logically separable elements: one factual and modal element and one recommendatory or normative element. The normative element of practical necessity is not like a layer which can be peeled away from the concept's empirical content.

IV

In order to discover what our fundamental needs are without confusion, it is necessary to distinguish different kinds of need. In this section, I shall present two such distinctions, which arise from the circumstances in which we need, rather than from the antecedent of the need. These distinctions may not always be firm and sharp, but they are essential to any theory of need.

First, we should distinguish derivative and non-derivative needs. A derivative need is one which a person has by virtue of his needing something else. If the only way of obtaining food is to buy it, and if a person has a need for food, then he has a derivative need for money. Having money is necessary for the food necessary for survival. If a need is derivative, then this will show itself in one way the relevant need claim can be challenged. Suppose that A claims to need X and the recognised condition of this claim is that A's putative need for X is dependent on his need for Y. In such a case, we can show that A does not need X by showing that he does not in fact need Y. A needs a prescription to obtain the medicine he thinks he needs to be cured of a dangerous illness. In fact A does not need the medicine, since only a change of diet will cure him of his illness. He is thus mistaken in thinking that he needs the prescription.

If some needs are derivative, others must be non-derivative or basic. A has a basic need for X if and only if he needs X but not in virtue of his needing something else. When A needs X derivatively in order to V, the question 'But do you *need* to V?' is appropriate and to the point. But when A's need is non-derivative, this question must be somehow inappropriate and beside the point. Otherwise the need for X would have to be derivative after all, contrary to supposition. Suppose the question were appropriate, then it must be answered either affirmatively or negatively. If the question 'Does A need to V?' is to be answered affirmatively, then A's need for X will be derivative on this need to V. If the answer is negative, then A will not need X at all. Either way, if the question 'Do you need to V?' is appropriate, then A's need for X relative to V cannot be basic. It must be logically out of place to ask whether a person needs that which is specified by the antecedent of a basic need claim.

One might explain this as follows. All fundamental needs pertain to the avoidance of serious harm. The object of such a need must be something the lack of which is harmful to the subject. Consequently, the question 'Do you need X?' is akin to the question 'Is not-X harmful?' Now, the assertion 'harm is harmful' looks tautologous, but in fact involves a category mistake, as do the statements 'Courage is courageous' and 'Danger is dangerous'. We can conclude from this that the question 'Do you *need* to avoid serious harm?' itself involves a category mistake because of its essential similarity to the question 'Is harm harmful?' Similarly, if death is a species of harm, the question 'Do you *need* to survive?' is like asking 'Is death fatal?'

The only trouble with this explanation is that it assumes that all fundamental needs must pertain to serious harm. It is only given this assumption that we have shown that the avoidance of harm is not an appropriate object of a fundamental need, and that what we need to avoid harm is a basic, non-derivative need. We can vindicate the assumption by trying to answer the question 'What could be an appropriate antecedent for the normative claims "I *need* to avoid harm" and "I *need* to survive"?' In special situations survival and the avoidance of harm can be the object of a normative 'need' claim. By examining a situation where the question of needing to survive is appropriate, insight may be gained into why the question is usually inappropriate. In Tennessee Williams' *The Night of the Iguana*, there is an ageing poet about to die, who is pregnant with the last verse of the crowning poem of his life. In this context, the poet might have justifiably claimed the need to live on in order to finish his masterpiece. That this could be regarded as a special reason or justification for this continued survival can be seen by his willingness to say 'Now I am ready to die' once he has completed his work. Furthermore, the old poet should be willing to say the same if we show him that he does not need to live on, if, for example, he has already finished his poem and has forgotten that.

How does this example differ from what is normally the case? The normative claim 'I *need* to survive' says that my survival is important or practically necessary, and that this is because it is a necessary condition of something especially important, like the completion of a valuable poem. The denial 'You don't *need* to survive' says that your survival is not practically necessary, and that this is because it is not a necessary condition of something especially important. For the poet, the value of survival is need-based in this way, and consequently when he no longer has that need, he no longer has a special reason to continue living, and he should say 'Now I no longer *need* to survive'. This is different from the normal case, because the value of life and the reason we have to avoid death is not in general due to the fact that living is necessary for any particular purpose, like the completion of a piece of work. Unlike the old poet, our reason to avoid death is not need-based. If I claim that I *need* to survive, the implication is that my survival is important because it is necessary for the completion of some task or goal. Similarly, the claim 'I don't *need* to survive' implies that my survival is not important because it is not necessary for the completion of some valuable task or goal. The normal value of life is not so specific, not dependent on the importance of particular purposes, and is not so easily forgone. This is why the question 'Do you *need* to survive?' and its affirmative and negative answers are normally inappropriate and beside the point.

It is no reply to this argument to contend that there are many true instances of the schema 'In order to V, A needs to survive'. Of course, survival is a necessary condition of each of life's activities, but this does not mean that we have a need to survive, because 'need' statements do not necessarily indicate needs. In order for there to be a normative need to survive, the following must be true: there must be some value for Y such that the normal personal importance of an individual's survival is non-trivially due to the fact

20

that his survival is necessary for Y. The failure to find a suitable value of 'Y' shows that the normal reason we have to avoid death is because of what death is, and not because we need to avoid it.

To conclude: in normal circumstances the questions 'Do you *need* to survive?' and 'Do you *need* to avoid serious harm?' are logically inappropriate, because they involve a category mistake akin to the category mistake involved in the questions 'Is death fatal?' and 'Is harm harmful?' Thus, in normal circumstances, what we need in order to survive and avoid serious harm are basic or non-derivative fundamental needs. In special situations we can *need* to survive and avoid harm, in order to complete some special task. In these special cases the need to survive and avoid harm are not fundamental needs because they do not non-trivially pertain to the subject's own welfare, but they are normative needs because they pertain to projects and goals which are important in some broad sense. When someone like the old poet needs to survive, the food and medicine which are necessary to keep him alive are objects of derivative or non-basic needs.

The distinction between basic and non-basic or derivative needs should not be confused with the difference between constitutional and circumstantial needs. In the schema for 'A needs X in C', 'C' stands for a description of the circumstances in which A needs X, or more precisely for the range of circumstances in which a relation of natural necessity holds between the two relevant states of affairs. These circumstances can be described in different ways, and this variation will affect the description that should be given of the object of need. For example, these circumstances can be described so that they are internal to the person who has the need, or part of his constitution, rather than any special situation that he happens to be in. Man needs food because of his physical make-up. If he is in a special situation in which there is no other food but bread available, we can say that he needs bread, where this need is relative to those special circumstances. Outside those circumstances, the claim 'man needs bread' will be false because it is overspecific. The need for food can be called 'a constitutional need' and the need for bread 'a circumstantial need'. A constitutional need is, in a sense, a need whatever the circumstances: it is a need that a person carries around with him from situation to situation.

If we confused these two types of need, then we might challenge what is in fact a circumstantial need claim on the grounds that it does not indicate a constitutional need, and conclude wrongly that the claim failed to indicate a need at all. For instance, the need for money is peculiar to certain social arrangements, and it is no argument against this assertion that in the past people could manage without money. In connection with this, it should be noted that, although many circumstantial needs will be derivative, basic needs can be circumstantial as well. If the need for food is basic then the need for bread, specific to circumstances in which bread is the only available food, is also a basic or non-derivative need. The need for bread may be both circumstantial and basic.

However, there is a sense of the term 'basic' in which all constitutional needs are basic. Often when we speak of a person's basic needs, we refer to those needs which he has by virtue of his make-up. When we say that people have a basic need for food, we mean that it is by virtue of their make-up that they must die without food. In this sense of the term 'basic', we do not have a basic need to avoid harm, and what we need non-derivatively in order to survive and avoid harm are the objects of basic needs.

II

HUMAN NATURE

Effugere non potes necessitates.
Naturam quidem mutare difficile est.

Seneca[1]

I

The Stoics are famous for distinguishing between aspects of our life that can and cannot come under our control.[2] People must apply this distinction in their everyday lives in order to make themselves less vulnerable to misfortune and frustration and to achieve ataraxia or tranquillity. To find tranquillity, man must live according to nature. Since nature's demands are few,[3] Stoics like Epictetus advocate a form of asceticism according to which man should only satisfy his true natural needs and should limit the artificial creation of false needs.

The Ancient philosophers were not especially interested in analysing the concepts of need and nature on which they relied. Indeed, ancient wisdom did not distinguish need and drive, and confused the necessity inherent in the concept of a need with the compulsion inherent in the notion of a drive.[4] Nevertheless, by following vaguely Stoic themes, we may come to a deeper understanding of the concept of a fundamental need and its links with human nature. Taking up the suggestion of Seneca, I shall argue that fundamental needs are inescapable. Two arguments will force us to this conclusion. First, the paradigm that fundamental needs are all inescapable, and this inescapability is essential to the way the concept of a fundamental need functions in practical reasoning. Thus, it is essential to the concept that we cannot give up our fundamental needs.

Secondly, it is vital to any account of the concept of a fundamental need that a distinction be drawn between our needs, on the one hand, the addictions and dependences, on the other. This distinction requires that our fundamental needs be inescapable. A third point: it is an old and hardy, but rather obscure, intuition that our basic fundamental needs are a natural feature of our make-up. The true meaning and importance of this intuition can again only be understood with reference to the claim that fundamental needs are inescapable.

The best way to explain what it means to say that a need is inescapable is through the notion of self-alteration. Self-alteration is an activity engaged in when a person does something to bring about a change in himself. For instance, a person can act to bring about changes in his talents, his desires, his feelings, what he finds enjoyable . . . Self-alteration is important for both morality and prudence. It can be, for example, a pre-condition of moral progress. Moral progress can require an active and intentional move to become more virtuous in character. This is because the scope of moral criticism includes not only what we do, but also why we do it. Similarly, prudence covers more than the expediency of particular acts, like looking before one crosses the road. Prudence often requires us to change the kind of persons we are, so that, for instance, we become less bitten by worry.

The possibility of self-alteration depends on two general features of the human organism. First, whether we intend it or not, what we do influences what we are.[5] By breaking more and more promises and engagements, I become less reliable, more disposed to act unreliably in the future. This causal reinforcing of character traits is all the more acute when those traits come in clusters rather than atomistically, because then there is a snow-balling effect: the more miserable I become, the more I have to complain about and, the more I complain, the more miserable I become. Unchecked action tends to emphasise dominant character traits at the expense of more latent ones. Some forms of self-alteration (S–A) can be regarded as the attempt to arrest this causal reinforcing and to redirect or steer if for the better. Secondly, S–A requires self-knowledge. In order to change oneself, one must be self-aware, and also aware of how certain changes in the world will affect one's character. If a person seeks to change himself, this must be because some feature of his personality appears undesirable. This self-awareness must be value-laden.

S-A should not be confused with various allied concepts. Altering oneself, and especially one's desires, should not be confused with resisting those desires. Resisting one's desires is one possible form of self-alteration, a type of training, but it is not the only form of S–A. Furthermore, a person can exercise self-restraint, not as a form of S–A, but simply to prevent himself doing something best not done: the desert-trecker resists his desire to drink the contaminated water. Self-alteration should also be distinguished from voluntary control. A person can alter one of his characteristics, without that being directly within the scope of his voluntary control or immediate will. Although I can blink at will, I can only change the size of my pupils by doing something to effect that change, such as looking into a bright light. Imagine two sorts of chameleon: those that can change their colouring at will, and those that have to go into the appropriately coloured environment.

To say of a characteristic that it cannot be changed by S–A is not to say that it is fixed and cannot change at all. A person cannot change the natural colouring of his hair, but as we grow older we grow greyer. Many features of our personality change as we grow older, and yet we cannot change them ourselves. They are not amenable to S–A, and the change is natural, something that we can do little about.

Although the concept of S–A is worthy of study in its own right, its opposite is more directly relevant to my immediate aims. The idea that there are natural limits to the extent to which we can change ourselves is of central importance to values generally, and is more specifically a key to the concept of a fundamental need. In the idea that there are natural limits to effective S–A, we find the confluence of two very general aspects of human nature. In actively and intentionally doing things to change ourselves, we are supremely agents and initiators of free action. We are the responsible masters of ourselves and the pilots of our own fate. But, in recognising that there are limits to S–A, we must acknowledge that we are not absolutely free to be and do as we like. In this sense, we have a human nature over which we have only limited control and choice.

This is an important theme recurrent throughout this book although the freedom to act and choose is a necessary condition of morality and prudence, the fact that we are not wholly free with respect to our own nature is also, as I shall argue, a necessary condition of rationality. Not only are persons free agents, but they are also beings with a nature, over which they have only limited control and choice.

In specifying the limits to effective S–A, we must be careful to make the specification factually precise. First, it must be stated exactly which characteristics or dispositions cannot be altered, and in what way they cannot. The need for water can be reduced, but it cannot be totally given up or reduced indefinitely. The felt strength of a desire may be reduced, its intentional object may be altered, but perhaps the general motivational force of the desire may remain inalterable. Secondly, we must give temporal constraints in our specification. What can be changed in the long run may be recalcitrant in the short-term. Thirdly, we must specify by what means a characteristic is or is not alterable. A disposition that can be changed in one way may be inalterable by some other means. Billy Bunter may be unable to give up his excessive desire for cake by reflecting on the miseries that this desire causes him, but may be able to do so with some sort of therapy. It is vital to specify the means by which a disposition is or is not alterable, because different means can have differing rational or moral significance. For instance, if a need is only alterable by some means which is harmful to the person concerned, then this may not count against the claim that the need is inescapable. In other words, some means of S–A may be discountable on moral or prudential grounds. If a person can only rid himself of his need for friendship by turning himself into a maniac killer in the process, this will not count against the assertion that the need for friendship is inescapable or cannot be changed by S–A.

When it is claimed that a need is inescapable, this does not mean then that the need is strictly inalterable. A need may be either so difficult to alter, or the cost so high on moral or prudential grounds, that for practical purposes, the need may be regarded as inalterable. A need is inescapable either if it is literally inalterable, or if the alteration is in some way discountable. If a person needs friendship, it does not count against the claim that this need is inescapable, if we can rid the person of his need by torturing him, causing him brain damage, or turning him into a psychopath. Note, also, that an inescapable need is not necessarily fixed. A need is inalterable if the person can do nothing to give up his need or if it does not come within the range of things that he can change. Quite compatible with this, the need may change by itself as he grows older. Therefore, the claim that our fundamental needs are inescapable in no way implies a static view of human nature. It only entails that some changes concerning our needs cannot be controlled.

Why should we acknowledge that our fundamental needs are inescapable? First, paradigm fundamental needs are inescapable: we cannot escape the fact that we must ail and eventually die without food, water, and air. Inescapability is not an accidental feature of those needs, because this feature is essential to the way the concept of a fundamental need functions as a value in reasoning. The objects of fundamental needs are necessary in the full-blooded sense of the term: these are things that we cannot do without, or that we must have. This means that on pain of death or some other form of serious harm, we have no alternative but to obtain what we need. We are forced to two alternatives: to eat or to die. There can be no other alternative, and since death is so bad, there is point and force in saying that we *must* eat. 'Need' applies to cases in which we have only two alternatives. Moreover, it is integral to the concept of a fundamental need that the reasons against one of these alternatives are so strong that, in most circumstances, we have no option but to try to obtain what we need. This explains the force of practical necessity accruing to the concept of a fundamental need, why we must have and cannot do without what we need. In brief, the logic of 'need' is such that it applies to cases in which our choice is restricted to only two alternatives, the reasons against one of these being so strong, that we have no practical or rational alternative but to seek what we need. This cutting down of choice could not work if we could easily escape our needs. If we could change the fact that without food we must die, then we would no longer be forced into the deadlock, only-two-options situation, of 'eat or die'. There would be a way out, and 'I must eat' or 'I *need* food' would be false. In so far as the statement 'I need food' implies that food is practically necessary, that I have no option but to obtain food, the statement would be false, if I could easily alter the fact that food is necessary for my survival. Changing myself would be a practical alternative to finding food, and thus food would not be a necessity. To conclude: the concept of a fundamental need restricts the viable courses of action down to only one, that is seeking what we need. This is why self-alteration is impossible with regard to our fundamental needs, and why these needs are inescapable. Consider an alien being for whom light is necessary for survival so long as the being has constitution C. Suppose that some organism can alter that aspect of its constitution with impunity. It could then adapt itself to long periods of darkness and survive them without suffering harm. Therefore, although light is necessary for its survival given C, light cannot be one of the organism's fundamental needs, because it can survive without it.

There is another reason for thinking that our fundamental needs are inescapable. An analysis of 'need' should include some distinction between needs and dependences/addictions, and this distinction requires the thesis that fundamental needs are inescapable. A person can be dependent on a substance to the extent that he cannot live without it, and yet he may not have a need for the substance. Put simply, dependences and addictions can be given up, but needs cannot. Given suitable time and treatment a person can be weaned off a dependence or addiction. In the case of an addiction, he has reason to be cured of his dependence, because the object of an addiction is harmful. An addiction is a curable dependence on a harmful substance. Because addictions and other dependences can be given up and needs cannot, objects of needs should take priority over objects of addiction and dependence in the long term. In the short term, an addiction may be as recalcitrant as a need, in which case, *ceteris paribus*, and within that time period, it is equally important for the person to have a supply of both what he needs and what he is addicted to. For so long as he has the addiction and death is consequent on its frustration, he has no reason to prefer lacking what he needs to lacking what he is addicted to. However, in the long run, he can shed his addiction and that should be considered less important than the need.

The inescapability of needs can be determined from two perspectives, and so far we have only considered one of these. So far we have treated the inescapability of a need in a purely future-regarding way: from this perspective a need is inescapable if a person can do nothing in the future to change the fact that he has this need, given his present constitution. Once a person has acquired an inalterable need, it is irrelevant whether he could have avoided its acquisition. However, from the second more broad perspective, inescapability includes both inalterability and unavoidability. In this sense, a need is inescapable if there is nothing a person can do to escape it in the future, and if there was nothing he could have done in the past to have avoided its acquisition. It is from this broader perspective that we ask 'What do people need?' where the question is intended quite generally, abstracted from the vagaries of fate.

The distinction between needs and dependences/addictions varies according to the perspective from which we determine inescapability: what is a need from the purely future-regarding point of view can be dependence from the more general point of view. From the point of view of his own future, A needs X if he must die or ail without it, and if he can do nothing to change this fact. If an addict must die without his drug and his addiction is as recalcitrant as his need for water, then the drug must count as one of his needs. The fact that he could have avoided the addiction is irrelevant. The disposition is now as inalterable as his other needs, and since he must have both the drug and food to survive, both have equal prudential value for him, and both count as needs. It is only from the more general perspective that we can entertain the possibility that an addiction can be as deeply ingrained and inalterable as a need, and yet not be a need. For from this perspective, facts about the acquisition of dependences and needs become relevant. The difference beween a need and a deeply ingrained and inalterable dependence is that we cannot avoid acquiring our needs and can avoid acquiring dependences and addictions. Addictions and dependences can be avoided with impunity. For a youth whose friends are all addicts, addiction may seem unavoidable, but that is only given his special and peculiar surroundings, and once we abstract the judgment from these, and place the judgment in a wider context, these special surroundings seem the kind that we have reason to discount when we are trying to ascertain what human needs are.

Addictions are not to be confused with what have been called 'false needs'. Objects of addiction are in themselves harmful, but false needs are a species of dependence whose objects are not harmful. When a writer claims that society inculcates false needs in its members, he may mean one or both of two things. First, a person has false needs if he has false beliefs about his needs. Society inculcates false needs when the culture of that society leads its members to have false beliefs about what their needs are, especially when that inculcation is necessary to the functioning and perpetuation of that culture in ways that are oppressive to individuals. Take a hypothetical example: suppose that the majority of people falsely believed that they need to have plastic around them, in their homes and on their shelves, for their well-being, and suppose that the whole economy and social structure depended on the manufacture of plastic, then plastic might be called 'a false need'. Secondly, a false need may be a species of dependence. A society creates false needs when the people who live and are reared in that society thereby acquire a real dependence that they would not have otherwise acquired. The false need is further marked by the fact that what leads to its acquisition is an oppressive or harmful feature of that society. To use the previous example: suppose that the majority of people in a society really were dependent on plastics for their well-being, but they only acquire this dependence because of an unhealthy consumer pressure on them, then plastic would be a false need in the second sense of the term. In this sense, a false need is a socially sanctioned dependence whose acquisition is harm dependent. Marcuse uses the phrase 'false need' in this second sense; he says:

> 'false' are those [needs] which are superimposed upon the individual by particular social interests in his repression.[6]

The concepts 'false need', 'addiction', and 'desire' are all distinct, although they are rarely distinguished. A false need of the first kind is an untrue belief that a person has about what he needs and thus is clearly not a form of addiction. False needs of the second kind are also not addictions, although like addictions they are a type of dependence. Whereas objects of addiction are harmful in themselves, objects of false need may not be. What is harmful about a false need is the environment that leads to its acquisition. Both false needs and addictions are different from our desires. The concept of an addiction is distinct from that of a desire, because a person does not have a desire to what he is addicted to, and many things that we desire we are not addicted to. The concept of false need is also distinct from that of a desire. False needs of the first kind are untrue beliefs about what we need. Although such false beliefs will generate appropriate desires, the two concepts are distinct. False needs of the second kind are a species of dependence, but being dependent on X is quite different from wanting it. So, even if in some political theories the desire/need distinction plays a similar role to the false/ true need distinction, we ought not to confuse these concepts. Finally, in what sense, if any, are false needs actually needs? In so far as false needs are real dependences relating to serious harm, rather than being untrue beliefs, and in so far as these dependences may become deeply ingrained and inalterable, then the individual must count his false needs among his fundamental needs. For, so long as he does not satisfy them he will be seriously harmed, and he can do nothing to alter this fact. He has reason to pay equal attention to the satisfaction of his true and false needs, all other things being equal. However, if he is aware of his false needs as such, then he will realise that what led to his acquiring them was a social force which was not in his interests, and that had society been different, he would not have had these false needs. This is the point of calling them '*false* needs'. In other words, he will regard his deeply embedded false needs as indelible blots on his nature put there by harmful social forces.

II

Throughout the history of thought philosophers have had the idea that our needs are a part of our nature. For example, this idea can be found in the writings of Seneca, Lucretius, Rousseau and Marx.[7] But it has never been clear what this idea amounts to and why it is supposed to be important. Furthermore, this idea has not received much close scrutiny in the modern tradition of analytic philosophy, except by way of some very general and often critical remarks on the concept of human nature. It is now time for this idea to receive some preliminary study, especially in view of the recent advent of sociobiology and psychogenetics, which mark a revived interest in the study of man.

When Butler sought to explain what he meant by saying that to be virtuous is to act in accordance with one's own nature, he began by citing what he did not mean by 'nature', and so shall I.

'Nature' can be used in an inclusive sense so that any feature of a person's personality is a part of his nature. Since this use does not effect any classification of needs into natural and non-natural needs, this use can be ignored. Secondly, a person's nature can be the behaviourally dominant features of his character, as when we say that it was the nature of Molière's M. Arnauld to be miserly. Like Butler, I mention this use to exclude it.

The spirit of what is meant by calling a need natural is that the need is innately rather than environmentally and socially determined. However, this statement is far too easily misconstrued, because it suggests a direct opposition between innate and socially determined, as if a need or any disposition had to be one or the other, but could not be both. This leads to the radically mistaken picture that man has an unchanging essential nature, and that the rest of his personality is a social garb. This kind of picture has done much to discredit the notion of human nature.[8] The root of this error is the belief that a disposition is innate only if it is in no way acquired or socially and environmentally determined. But genes do not unconditionally determine any characteristics of an organism. The effects of genetic structure are always relative to the organism's upbringing, social environment, and past actions. Take, for instance, the ability to learn a language: it is not genetically determined that humans are language users; it is genetically determined that *if* a human baby is subject to the right kind of environment and social conditions, then it will have the ability to learn a language. We can only understand the innate nature of an organism by seeing how it responds, and what its capabilities are in different environmental and social conditions. Our innate nature determines within broad limitations what we are like in different social settings. The only way of knowing what our innate nature consists of is through the way we are in different social settings, because that is what our innate nature is. Thus, it is radically mistaken directly to oppose 'innate' to 'socially determined'. This is not because the effects of our inheritance and environment are finely intertwined, but because in a sense they are inseparable. Our genetic nature is just the way we are variously affected by different social conditions.

What then does it mean to say that a need is natural? If we say that a need is natural if it is innately rather than socially determined, this seems to involve the confusions that we have already exposed. It seems to require the blanket opposition of innate and social factors that we have condemned. However, what is meant by calling a need 'natural' is roughly this: that the person or organism does not have his need because he was brought up in some special way, and that he would still have had the need if he had been brought up in a different way. A simple hypothetical experiment can illustrate how we might test whether a disposition is natural or not and to what degree. We take several individuals of the same genotype and rear groups of them differently, controlling these differences as much as we can. If two individuals differ with respect to some characteristic, then this difference must be traced to the differing conditions in which they were reared. If certain characteristics are shared by all the individuals concerned, no matter how they were brought up, then this may count as evidence that the characteristic is innate. More precisely, if more of the organisms have feature F than feature P, then F is more genetically determined than P relative to that range of environmental conditions for that genotype.

We cannot automatically conclude from this, however, that F is more natural than P for organism O. The model or hypothetical experiment yields judgments as to whether a characteristic of an organism is more genetically determined than another for a genotype relative to a range of environmental influences. There may be a hidden bias in the parameter 'relative to a range of environmental influences' which prevents us from going on to conclude that F is more natural than P for organism O. In order to conclude this, the range of environmental influences to which the organisms are subject in our hypothetical experiment must be both varied enough and of the right kind. The range of environmental influences must be varied, because to get a picture of whether a disposition is natural for an organism, we need a broad overview of the effects of its genetic structure in a wide range of environmental conditions. If we restrict the test to a very confined range of environmental influences, then the test will be too parochial for us to make any conclusions about what is natural for the organism. When Margaret Mead allegedly discovered that adolescents in New Guinea do not suffer the same problems as they do in Western culture, she discovered that those problems were less natural than we thought them to be. Had it been the case that adolescents in any culture suffer these problems, then we might have concluded that those problems were natural for adolescents, more on par for instance, with the ability to learn a language or the disposition to play. In any case, it would be wrong to jump to conclusions about what is natural for humans simply by studying their behaviour and dispositions in our culture. To make judgments about what is in our nature, we require an overview of the effects of our genetic structure in a wide

33

and varied range of environmental conditions.

In order to judge whether a characteristic is natural for an organism, given the type of hypothetical experiment described earlier, two conditions must be met. The range of environmental influences to which the organism is subject in the experiment must be both varied and of the right kind. Some environmental conditions can be discounted because they are of the wrong kind. For example, we can discount from the experiment environmental influences which are harmful to the organism, because we would not wish to call a need 'natural', if that need was only acquired in circumstances that were harmful to the organism.

A need is natural *par excellence* when the organism would have that need in all non-discountable social and environmental conditions. This definition links natural needs and inescapability. The definition entails that a need is natural when it is inescapable, i.e. inalterable and unavoidable, for beings of a particular genotype. For if a baby will later acquire a need-disposition whatever non-discountable social and environmental pressures it is subject to, then there is nothing non-discountable that can be done to change the fact that it will acquire the need. In other words, by virtue of being natural, the need is inescapable. On the other hand, if a need is avoidable and alterable, then there is a range of environmental and social conditions in which the organism does not have the need, and it is not natural. If it were easy to avoid acquiring a need disposition, then that disposition is *ipso facto* less natural, because this is evidence that it is accidentally acquired rather than genetically determined. Natural needs are features of our inherent make-up, and because of this they are inescapable. As an Englishman Seneca might have said, we cannot knead our natural needs.

III

HARM: OBJECTIVE OR SUBJECTIVE?

All is offence when a man has forsaken his true nature
and is doing what does not befit him.

Sophocles

I

James starts to feel tired, bored and depressed. He loses interest in his work and loses touch with his friends. He is snappy and uncommunicative with his wife who feels alienated and distressed. He spends more and more time watching television and reading cheap paperbacks. Finally, he begins to feel despair and starts to drink.

Beings on planet Kakapos live routine and ordered lives. Each part of their day is allocated to serve a particular kind of interest. Having special auditory tastes, they spend the morning singing to themselves. At noon they rest and sit absorbing sunlight through their large green ears. Sunlight is their only source of nourishment. Throughout the rest of the day they sleep or watch the clouds drift. Despite the fact that they seem contented and would say that they are, these beings are living at half-mast. A regular vegetable diet would dramatically improve the quality of their lives: they would find the energy to be more social, to take more care of their young, to practise their singing communally as an art, to explore and travel.

The central pillar of any analysis of the concept 'fundamental need' must be a characterisation of its antecedent, i.e. what the object of a fundamental need is necessary for – the avoidance of serious harm. If a person lacks what he needs, the quality of his life must suffer. Both of the examples cited on the previous page illustrate how the quality of a life might be impaired or how a person's well-being might be harmed. However, there are crucial differences between the two examples and the way in which they have a bearing on 'need'. It is debatable whether James lacks something he needs. If a person lacks what he needs then he must suffer serious harm, in the sense that the quality of his life must be impaired, and will continue to be impaired until he has what he needs. It is not clear that James lacks one thing without which he cannot recover. He may be able to arrest his decline in many ways. Moreover, he may be suffering a temporary misfortune which will right itself. In so far as it relates to need, harm is not merely a temporary misfortune, but is a permanent degeneration in the quality of life which must continue until we have what we need. Therefore, in relation to fundamental needs, temporary misfortunes of the kind James may be suffering do not count as serious harm. On the other hand, beings from Kakapos do lack something they need. As long as they lack a vegetable diet, they must continue to live in low gear. They cannot recover from this harm without it.

The first example shows how a person can suffer harm without being in need. The second example illustrates two features of the concept 'need', which may otherwise escape our attention. First, it illustrates that we may never have had what we need, and thus do not necessarily undergo an actual decline in the quality of our lives when we lack what we need. In so far as 'harm' relates to 'need', it does not necessarily indicate a drop or fall in the quality of life because it can indicate a continuing low quality of life. The poor who have never had money are deprived and harmed, even though their standard of living has never actually fallen.

The second example also illustrates that harm need not be felt. The beings from Kakapos do not realise that they are badly off. They do not feel depressed, miserable, bored or in pain as a consequence of lacking what they need. Therefore, harm does not necessarily involve intrinsically bad states of mind. This suggests that harm should be regarded as a type of deprivation rather than as a state of mind. It suggests that something harms us when it deprives us of the more valuable aspects of living. This is a signifi-cant point because it determines how one ought to approach the problem of analysing the concepts 'harm' and 'need'. Any account of 'need' must involve a characterisation of harm, and this characterisation must reveal what kind of reason we have to avoid harm. If harm is primarily a type of deprivation, then this characterisation of the disvalue of harm must show why the things we are deprived of when we are harmed are good or valuable. In other words, the emphasis of the analysis must be on explaining why certain types of activities and experiences are intrinsically valuable or desirable.

Some philosophers will resist this emphasis on explaining the intrinsically desirable at the expense of the intrinsically undesirable.[1] Harm can and often does involve intrinsically undesirable states of mind, like feeling miserable and being in pain. It might be argued, therefore, that harm need not consist in the absence of intrinsic goods, because it can consist in the presence of intrinsic evils. Treating harm primarily as a deprivation of intrinsic goods ignores the obvious fact that there are intrinsic evils, like pain and depression, and that these are a common ingredient of harm. Thus, in analysing the concept of harm, we cannot concentrate on explaining the intrinsically good at the expense of the intrinsically bad. In reply to this argument, notice that the evil of negative states of mind partly lies outside their felt quality. It is a common error to believe that the badness of pain consists solely in the fact that we dislike it. But pain is also bad because it is incapacitating and disrupts the course of life. Severe pain cripples, and even a little pain prevents us from appreciating the value of what we are doing. Like other negative states of mind, pain is bad not only because it is natively disliked, but also because of what it prevents us from doing, enjoying and appreciating. This implies that pain is in part a form of deprivation, and that to explain the negative value of states of mind like pain, we must also explain the positive value of the things which pain prevents us from doing and appreciating. Therefore, we are right to emphasise the problem of explaining harm as a form of deprivation and to concentrate on explaining the intrinsically good rather than the intrinsically bad, even when the latter *is* an ingredient of harm.

The view of harm as primarily a form of deprivation explains why harm need not be felt. It also explains why a person does not have to want to avoid harm in order to have reason to do so. It is neither necessary nor sufficient to want to avoid harm in order for harmful things to be worth avoiding. Harmful things have negative value simply because they deprive us of intrinsic goods, whether we want to avoid harm or not. This point is quite independent of the claim that harm is desire-based. Desire-based theories of harm do not claim that we must want to avoid harmful things in order for them to be worth avoiding. These theories claim that something harms us if it deprives us of things which are valuable in the sense that we desire them.

A deprivational view of harm also clarifies the relationship between need and survival. The need for food, water, and air are commonly thought to be among our basic fundamental needs. Yet people have a need for friendship even when it is clear that they will not die without it. So, survival needs can count as fundamental needs, and yet fundamental needs cover more than survival. Both of these points can be accommodated in a theory of fundamental needs given two assumptions: that fundamental needs pertain to the avoidance of serious harm, and that death can be a harm. Death is harm because it deprives us of life.[2]

As Nagel says:[3]

> If death is an evil it cannot be because of its positive features but only because of what it deprives us of.

If a person has a fundamental need for X then X is something he must have or cannot do without. What we need is practically necessary. Although the reason we have to seek what we need can be overridden in special circumstances, normally a person has no practical or rational alternative but to seek what he needs. To explain why needed things are practically necessary, we must analyse the content of the concept need, and in particular the antecedent of a need – the avoidance of serious harm. A theory of need must explain what harm is, and the ultimate goal of this explanation must be to show why we cannot do without what we need. If harm is a form of deprivation, then the route to this goal is clear. We must show why it is bad to be harmed by answering the following two questions:

1 When something harms us what does it deprive us of?
2 Why is what we are deprived of good?

The ultimate aim in answering these two questions is to explain why the concept of fundamental need includes an element of practical necessity because of its links with serious harm. However, not every absence or loss of a good counts as a harm; for instance, my going to the cinema tonight is a good, but if I am unable to go this does not constitute a harm. Thus to achieve our ultimate aim, the answers to the above questions should show when the absence of a good is and is not a harm.

It is easy to confuse the question 'Does the absence of X constitute harm?' with the question 'Is the absence of X harmful?' The two questions are different; the first does not concern what causes us harm, but what we are deprived of when something does cause us harm. The first question concerns what harm consists of and the second what harm is caused by. In order to properly appreciate this difference, we must distinguish primary and secondary value. Secondary value must be explained with reference to primary value.[4] For example, if we need X, then X is a secondary good, but the things we are deprived of when we lack X are ultimately primary goods. In this case, the value of the secondary good X is that it promotes or is necessary for certain primary goods. Another example: if Y is harmful then Y is a secondary evil because it deprives us of certain primary goods. Many activities and experiences are both primary and secondary goods, but it is still necessary to distinguish the two types of value. For instance, eating is an enjoyable activity and as such is a primary good. But eating is also a secondary good because it is necessary for life and health. Similarly, many of the activities recommended to us on the ground that they lead to health are also primary goods. Health itself is both a primary and a secondary good. If we concentrate on the secondary value of activities and experiences, then this merely postpones the question of their primary value. So it is to the question of their primary value that we should address ourselves: what kind of primary goods do harmful things deprive us of and why are they primary goods?

Despite the fact that we must concentrate on the question of primary goods, it is an important feature of the concept 'harm' that the things we are deprived of when we are harmed have both primary and secondary value. If something is both a primary and a secondary good, then it is doubly bad to lack it. Harm typically does reinforce itself in this way: the things we lack when we are harmed are things which are harmful to lack. In this sense, harm has an ongoing quality, and is the opposite of flourishing. The good things which we have and appreciate when we flourish themselves lead us on to further goods, and so on.

What are we deprived of when we are harmed? States of mind or states of the world?[5] According to the mental state theory of harm, only states of mind count towards the quality of a person's life; something harms us if it deprives us of desirable states of mind. It is natural to contrast this view with certain desire theories of harm, according to which anything we desire counts towards the quality of a person's life, because something harms us if it deprives us of things we urgently desire. Thus, according to these desire theories, being deprived of what we desire counts as harm, even if what we desire bears no relation to our states of mind.

Some versions of the mental state theory are framed in terms of pleasure and enjoyment: something enhances the quality of our lives if it causes us more pleasure and enjoyment, and detracts from the quality of life if it causes us to feel less pleasure and enjoyment. There are familiar problems with this type of view. First, it is a mistake to think that enjoyable activities are ones that cause us pleasure. Something desired because it is enjoyable may be desired for its own sake, and not as a means to enjoyment. Enjoyment should not be construed as a simple mental state over and above the activities and experiences we enjoy. Enjoyment is best thought of adverbially, as qualifying the way someone did or experienced something, rather than as a mental state caused by enjoyable activities. We enjoy ourselves when we like what we are doing.

Furthermore, the varied instances of enjoyable activities do not share one common felt quality, which they cause, and which can be singled out as enjoyment or pleasure. This is especially apparent granted the following observation. To say that an activity is enjoyable is to give it a very broad and general desirability characterisation, and the great variety of descriptions which fall under this general category do not apply to activities because they cause in us a single type of mental state. Enjoyment and pleasure are not mental states, but consist of liking and enjoying what one does. Therefore, the nature of enjoyment is not logically independent of what we enjoy: there is, for instance, the pleasure of having accomplished some difficult task, of watching one's children grow . . . Satisfactions are not identifiable independently of the kinds of things which satisfy us.

The hardest thing to swallow about the mental-state account is the claim that what we actually do, the activities we engage in, and what happens to us in the world do not count towards the quality of our lives. Surely, our well-being cannot be understood solely in terms of how we feel, and what we experience from the inner point of view. Nozick's experience machine makes the difficulty intuitively clear:[6] the machine will give you any experience you want; it will make you think that you are writing a masterpiece or falling in love when in fact you are floating in a tank with electrodes in your brain. From this example Nozick draws the conclusion that things other than our states of consciousness matter, namely what we are and do.

Nozick's example shows what is wrong with the mental-state account. However, it is misleading to conclude from this that what we actually do and undergo is valuable in addition to, or instead of, mental states. First, if what we are deprived of when we are harmed are desirable activities which we could have engaged in, and desirable happenings which we could have experienced, then these ingredients of harm already involve consciousness. Being conscious is already an integral part of doing, being and experiencing things in the world, in so far as these matter to the quality of our lives. The constituents of well-being are not states of awareness, but are activities and experiences which come within the ambit of awareness. For example, walking the dog is a worthwhile activity, but walking the dog in one's sleep is not.

Secondly, mental states do count towards the quality of life, but usually in so far as they arise from a proper appreciation of the actual value of what we are doing and undergoing. For instance, it is good to feel and be a success; something is amiss if a person feels a success but in fact is a failure, or if a person feels a failure whilst he is really a success. To live a desirable life one must experience and appreciate the value of what one does and undergoes. This means that something harmful can deprive a person in two ways. It may actually prevent him from engaging in activities which are primary goods, or it may prevent him from appreciating the value of what he is doing without actually preventing him from doing it. Being in prison prevents one from doing lots of things, but being depressed prevents one from enjoying, appreciating, and feeling the value of what one does.

These points do not vindicate the mental-state theory of harm. It still remains true that what we actually do and undergo counts towards the quality of life. Nevertheless, mental states are an integral part of our doing and experiencing things in the world, in so far as these matter to the quality of our lives.

This answer to the question 'what are we deprived of when we are harmed?' rules out the mental-state theory. It also rules out the type of desire theory mentioned earlier, according to which we are harmed when we are deprived of what we desire, even if that bears no relation to our awareness.[7] This type of theory has counter-intuitive results. It implies, for instance, that we can be harmed after our death. If Stravinsky wanted his music to be admired, then the beings from Kakapos who hate it thereby harm Stravinsky. It also implies that being loved by a person in Australia can count directly towards the quality of one's life, even if one has never heard of this love. Surely, what does count is being with someone who loves you and appreciating their love. Something which deprives us of secret lovers and unknown admirers does not harm us, even if it is good to be secretly admired and loved. Similarly, something which prevents our desires from being satisfied after we have died does not harm us, even if it is good to respect the wishes of the dead.[8] The desire theory should be rejected because something harms a person if it deprives him of primary goods which come within the ambit of the person's awareness. The posthumous frustration of desires does not qualify, therefore, as harm. Harm deprives us of elements of living, though some of our desires reach out beyond our lives.

Currently there is a lot of resistance to views which exclude the possibility of posthumous harm. This resistance is misguided. For instance, Feinberg argues that[9]

1 A person can be harmed during his life time by things which he does not know; for example, a man is harmed if his wife secretly betrays him, or if his good reputation is destroyed without his being aware of it.
2 If knowledge is not a necessary condition of harm during a person's lifetime, why should we think that it is necessary after his death?
3 If knowledge is not a necessary condition of harm either before or after death, then posthumous harm is possible.

The view I am urging, namely that we are harmed when we are deprived of the good elements of living, does exclude the possibility of posthumous harm. It does not, however, imply the principle 'What you don't know can't hurt you', as Feinberg suggests. Clearly, what we are not aware of can harm us; the unknown can be harmful. Also, we can be harmed without knowing this. But, contrary to what Feinberg says, the issue is not the relationship between awareness and what harms us, nor that between awareness and being harmed, but rather the relationship between awareness and what we are deprived of when we are harmed. Feinberg's argument misses the mark, because secret betrayal can cause us harm without our realising this, for instance, by making an important relationship less good than it would have been.

With regard to Feinberg's first premise above, the question is not 'Can secret betrayal harm a person?' but 'Can secret betrayal be an ingredient of harm, during the subject's life time?' It *can*, because a person who has been betrayed has lost the loyalty of a friend and to this extent, at least, one of his relationships is less good, even if he is not aware of this fact. A relationship which he has and experiences, and which forms an important element of his life, is now worse. Although he is not aware of the fact that it is worse, the thing which is worsened does come within the ambit of his awareness. Harm must impoverish what comes within the ambit of the subject's awareness, but it does not require that the subject is aware of that impoverishment.

Contrary to Feinberg's premise 2, there is a difference between secret betrayal which comes within the subject's life time and posthumous betrayal. As a consequence of this difference, the first can be an ingredient of harm and the second cannot. The difference is that normal betrayal impoverishes a relationship which a person is having and experiencing, but posthumous betrayal does not. The dead person no longer experiences and has the relationship which is impoverished; it is no longer an element of his life. Of course, this does not mean that it does not matter if we betray our dead friends, and ruin their reputation. It does mean that such acts do not cause harm to the dead and do not constitute harm to the dead.[10]

The point about awareness establishes what general categories of things we are deprived of when we are harmed, namely activities and experiences. In addition to this, harm is not the deprivation of particular activities, like playing golf next Sunday, nor is it usually the deprivation of specific types of activity, like playing golf, but it is the deprivation of very general types of activities and experiences, like sport or communal physical exercise. A man in prison might miss playing football every Sunday, but the harm he undergoes is

43

not so specific. It is not specifically football that he is deprived of, but any other communal physical activity he could have engaged in, as well as a whole host of other general types of activity. The fact that harm is the deprivation of general types of desirable activity helps us to explain why it is not the case that the absence of every good thing is a harm. Being deprived of particular good does not constitute harm, because the absence of a particular good is not serious when there are other particulars which can replace it. If I can't go to the cinema on Saturday, but I can go to the theatre on Tuesday or watch television with friends or go to dinner, then the loss of the cinema is not serious. On the other hand, being deprived of all forms of entertainment is a serious absence.

Earlier in this chapter, I stressed that any analysis of the concept 'fundamental need' must include an elucidation of the concept 'harm', and that since harm is primarily a form of deprivation, the analysis of 'harm' should answer the following questions:

1 When something harms us what does it deprive us of?
2 Why is what we are deprived of good?

So far we have concentrated on question 1. Now we must answer question 2. It is impossible to understand what harm is and what a fundamental need is without knowing in broad terms what general types of activities and experiences are primary goods or worthwhile to a person and why. We must explain why the primary goods we are deprived of when we are harmed are good or worthwhile. Here it is common practice to contrast subjectivist desire theories of harm and well-being with objectivist non-desire theories. I shall follow this general practice, and argue that both types of theory are inadequate. In the remainder of the chapter, I shall discuss the notion of a desire in order to tease out an alternative approach to the notions of harm and well-being, and to answer question 2.

II THE DESIRE ACCOUNT

According to the most simple version of the desire theory of harm and well-being, an event is harmful to a person's well-being if and only if it deprives him of things which are valuable to him in the sense that he desires them. It deprives him of certain primary goods, where the notion of a primary good or what is worthwhile to a person is elucidated in terms of the person's actual desires and preferences. However, this version of the desire account is too simple, because establishing that something is desired does not establish that it is a good. First, many of the things we desire are quite trivial and being deprived of them does not count towards harm. Furthermore, many things we desire are harmful to us, and being deprived of things which cause us harm does not count as a form of harm. Secondly, desires are typically at the mercy of the troughs and storms of changing emotions. Do the desires I have now in a fit of anger count towards my well-being, although my euphoria tomorrow will make them seem insignificant? Thirdly, we cannot include future desires in the theory without some form of assessment, for future and present desires may be in conflict. These criticisms of the simple desire theory may be generalised: we do distinguish a person's aims and desires being frustrated from the person himself being harmed and, if we are to capture this distinction within a desire theory of harm, desires must be subject to some form of assessment or criticism before they can be used to define the value of primary goods in a theory of well-being and harm.

The most obvious way of doing this seems to be to link well-being and harm to a person's *informed* desires: those desires he would have if he had certain information: if, for instance, he knew the implications of having what he wanted. So, according to this type of desire theory, an event is detrimental to a person's well-being if and only if it deprives him of things that he would desire or prefer if he were informed, where the value of those things is to be explained by the fact that he would desire them, i.e. in terms of informed desire satisfaction.[11]

Of course, this is not yet a full-blown theory of harm, for the informed desire theorist has to provide some account of the notion of the strength of informed desires and some way to rank present and future informed desires when these conflict. However, it seems premature to see these problems as a reason for rejecting the informed desire account, unless there is reason to believe that these difficulties in principle cannot be overcome.[12] Rather than concentrating on this line of enquiry, I wish to challenge the basic starting place of the desire theorist, his contention that the primary value relevant to harm is constituted by informed desire satisfaction – that something's being worthwhile to a person and it's being the object of an informed desire of his, amount to the same thing.

Note, as a preliminary point, that the informed desire account can be made more substantial. Suppose that in a situation of competing options A forms a clear-sighted preference for one of the alternatives. To know what is in A's interest with regard to his personal welfare, we need only know what his informed preference is for. But, granted that, matters do not end here: there is more to be known. To have a substantial understanding of A's well-being, we would also have to know on the basis of what information A forms his preference. There is a counter-factual story to be told about how A would prefer one alternative when possessed of certain information, and how he would change his mind on acquiring new pieces of knowledge. Knowing that X will improve his chances of becoming wealthy A prefers X, but on learning that X will involve a sacrifice of his family life and that wealth will not make him happy, A prefers option Y. This kind of information gives us a better substantial understanding of what A's well-being consists of. This supplement, however, does nothing to refute the formal claim that prudential value is best understood in terms of informed desire satisfaction. It merely provides a way of adding flesh to that formal account.

However, the supplement highlights a problem for the informed desire account. Suppose that person A is inclined to do X, but on learning that X will make him horribly sick, his preference changes for a harmless option Y. As the story has been so far told, Y is better for A than X, but the fact that A, knowing this, actually prefers Y to X, seems definitionally irrelevant to the greater desirability of Y or X. The fact that his informed preference is for Y rather than X is explained by the preferability of Y over X, and hence it cannot constitute that preferability. What makes the one course of action more preferable for A than the other is the facts about the options, and not A's preference once he is informed of those facts. The facts explain and justify his informed preference: A perceived the greater value of Y and his preferences changed accordingly. A's change in preference merely indicates his sensitivity to the different preferability of the options, therefore they are not constitutive of that preferability, but merely reflect it.[13]

If informed desires do not constitute what is in a person's interests, but merely reflect that, then we should expect that sometimes his informed preferences should reflect his interests poorly. This will be the case when a person's informed preference is for the less desirable of two options. The informed desire theorist holds that Y's being a greater value than X for A is constituted by A's having an informed preference for Y rather than X. Thus, the theorist cannot admit one counter-example to this formal claim. One counter-example where A knowingly prefers the less desirable of two options, where informed preference and prudential preferability are not co-extensive, is enough to dash the theory to the ground. Suppose I desire to smoke, and that, when I learn about all the damaging effects of smoking, I still desire to smoke. My informed preference is to smoke rather than not, even though the health risks outweigh the pleasures of smoking. I may even believe that it is better for me to stop smoking, although my informed preference is to continue.

If a person can have an informed desire for something which is not to his benefit, this is because his preferences need not be sensitive to his perception of the facts. This is confirmation of the previous claim, that informed preferences are to be explained by the relative desirability of their objects and therefore cannot constitute that desirability. The relationship between 'being of greater value to A' and 'being the object of A's informed preference' is such that A's perception of the first will be the cause of the second. If that is so, then they cannot amount to the same thing, and if they do not amount to the same thing, then it is possible for there to be extensional differences between them.

The desire theorist will have to argue that such extensional differences are impossible. Thus he must insist that if A prefers X to Y when Y is of greater value than X, then A's preference cannot be of the right kind, in order that this should not count as a counter-instance to the theory. Thus, in the cigarette example, although the person knows that it is worse for him to smoke, he continues to prefer this because he does not fully appreciate the harm. If he did appreciate it, he would not prefer to smoke. So, 'informed desire' should mean 'a desire a person would have were he to appreciate this information'. The desire theorist will claim, that so defined, informed desires will coincide with our interests

In order to assess this claim, we require a non-circular definition of 'appreciation'. It is circular to define 'appreciation' in terms of our informed preferences matching what is valuable, e.g. a person appreciates what he prefers if and only if he prefers Y to X only when Y is more valuable than X.

Harm: objective or subjective?

The problem is that we do have an independent grip on the notion of being informed, but the definition of prúdential value in terms of informed preference was open to counter-example. Without an independent grip on the substitute notion of appreciation in the phrase 'what a person would prefer if he appreciated what it is like to have what he prefers', it advances us no further to define prudential value in terms of this phrase.

Lear says 'wisdom and goodness to the vile seem vile.' This suggests that a person's character or emotional state may prevent him from appreciating the import of what he knows. The desire theorist may wish to follow this suggestion by trying to specify the conditions which prevent a person from appreciating what is best for him, and thus preferring what is best for him. For instance, Frey suggests defining utility or welfare in terms of rational desire satisfaction. He defines rational desires as:

> those desires we would have if we were not at present angry or under stress or under the influence of drink or suffering from depression and if we were rational, if we possessed knowledge of ourselves . . . and if we possessed sufficient detachment to assess such knowledge and information calmly and carefully.[14]

We may wonder whether even this list is complete; surely an indefinite number of things could prevent us from properly appreciating what we desire, and thus prevent us from desiring what is best. It seems hopeless to define the prudentially good by trying to enumerate all the ways in which a person can desire the prudentially bad. Perhaps some versions of the desire theory escape this particular criticism. We should distinguish the choices of a hypothetical person from the hypothetical choices of an actual person. Frey leans towards the former when he seeks to define well-being in terms of desires which are largely ideal. But, rather than relying on the preferences of knowing, detached and sensible expert, we might appeal to the hypothetical desires of the actual person whose well-being is under consideration, whether or not he is a cool, sensitive type. Rather than appealing to ideal desires, we might appeal to desires which are actual when fulfilled: such that when the object of desire obtains, the desire remains actual.[15] But now the theory looks too close to the simple actual desire account. For under the influence of fear, ambition, worry I may be glad of things which are to my detriment or not be glad of things which clearly are to my benefit. Things which are bad for us can be attractive to us and our desires for them can remain actual when fulfilled. We can desire something which is bad for us and at the time know that it is bad for us.

In order to avoid these problems the desire theorist will have to say that the person's subjective preferences do not match what is best for him because the preferences are not of the right kind. The person knows that what he desires is harmful but he cannot fully appreciate the harm, for if he did his desire would be different. But now, we are back to the problem of how to give a non-circular definition of 'appreciation', without trying to list all the ways in which a person can fail to properly appreciate the options before him.

However much we juggle with the notion of an informed preference, it seems to be merely a general contingent truth subject to counter-instances that people's informed desires are for the prudentially good. Because this is a contingent truth subject to exceptions, we cannot define the primary value relevant to harm in terms of informed desire; the latter cannot constitute the former. This confirms and reinforces the earlier argument that a person's change in preference, subsequent to his acquiring information, can be explained and justified in terms of the factual content of this information, and thus it is the factual content of the information, rather than the change in preference that constitutes the prudential preferability.

All of this lends a new angle to our very first point.[16] This was that to have a substantial understanding of a person's well-being, we will need to know on the basis of what general information concerning himself and the world a person will form clear-sighted preferences. But now it seems that knowing what this information is will not always be a supplement to knowing what a person's informed preferences are, but will at least sometimes usurp the latter. Knowing on what basis A will form clear-sighted preferences will replace knowing what those clear-sighted preferences are, when those preferences are to be explained and justified by that basis.

III THE OBJECTIVE ACCOUNT

Talking about moral desirability, Platts says 'things are so independently of our desires'.[17] Extending his position to prudential desirability, we arrive at what might be called 'an objective conception of well-being'. Well-being is independent of our desires: whether some event is detrimental to a person's well-being depends on whether that event deprives the person of activities and experiences that are truly characterised by certain desirability predicates and does not depend on the person's desires actual or possible.

The underlying motivation for this view is a thesis about the role of desires in action explanation and justification. Platt is a clear exponent of this thesis, so I shall follow his exposition, although it is not directed explicitly to harm, well-being and prudential desirability. The thesis about desires and reasons for action is developed by repudiating a dogma from philosophical psychology. The dogma is that 'any complete specification of even a prima facie reason for action must make reference to the potential agent's desires or possible desires'. Platts attacks this dogma, which he says is incompatible with moral realism,[18] by developing a thesis which explains why desires are reasons for action. He contrasts desire with pain. It is the essential phenomenological component of pain, the painfulness of pain, which silences the question 'Why should that motivate?' However, most desires lack a comparable phenomenological component and, unlike pains, desires have a logical object. So, according to Platts, the motivating force of a desire derives from its logical object or content. Desires motivate an agent because of his view of the object of his desire as independently desirable. Desirability is prior to desire, says Platts, because a desire for X needs explaining with reference to the independent desirability of X. The desirability of X is independent of desire because the agent's desires do not account for any desirability attributed to the object of desire.

So an objective account of well-being is underpinned by a thesis about the role of desires in action explanation and justification. The thesis says that an action is not explained by the mere citing of a desire; the act of desiring as such does not confer intelligibility on an action, because desires themselves need explaining. A desire is made intelligible by the fact that its object answers to a desirability characterisation. It is the fact that the object is describable in this way, and not the fact that it is wanted, that constitutes a reason for action and a value. Hence, it is argued that the notion of wanting can be allowed to fall out altogether from an account of reasons for action.[19] The concept of desire has no place in a theory of reasons since all we require is the notion of desirability. It is a short step from this general position to the more specific view that desire has no place in a theory of well-being and harm.

Platts' exposition suffers from a crucial and simple confusion common to most objectivist theories. He fails to distinguish a plausible weak thesis from an implausible stronger thesis. The weak thesis is the denial of a dogma from philosophical psychology. The weak thesis denies the dogma that any complete specification of a prima facie reason for action A must make reference to the potential agent's desire to do A. The weak thesis asserts that an agent can have a reason to do A without desiring to do A. Platts must assert and argue for this weak thesis in order to defend his realism, for the realist contends that judgments about what we have reason to do can transcend our recognition: that an action can be desirable without the potential agent recognising that.

The weak thesis says that the desirability of action A can be independent of an actual desire for A. The strong thesis says that the desirability of A must be independent of any desire, actual or possible. The reason for the strong claim is that desires are redundant in action explanation and justification, because desirability is prior to and independent of desire, whether actual or possible. The strong claim thus has the consequence that no desire (with the possible exception of phenomenological desires like lust) can itself be a reason for action.

The two claims are clearly distinct, and there are several intermediate positions between them (I would say that the weak thesis is true and the strong one false, though I shall not argue for that now). To defend realism, Platts need argue only for the weaker thesis, but he presents his arguments in favour of the stronger claim.

Even an ardent subjectivist can accept the weaker Nagelian type thesis that person P can have a reason to do A without his desiring to do A.[20] In the case of explanatory reasons, this being because he believes that A is desirable and in the case of guiding reasons, this being because A actually is desirable. The subjectivist can also accept the slightly stronger claim that if a person has a reason to do A this cannot be because he desires to do A. All the subjectivist need add is that the desirability of A is to be formally explained in terms of actual or possible desires. In the case where A is morally desirable, the desirability is to be explained in terms of actual or possible desires which are not the agent's own desires, but someone else's. In the case where A is prudentially desirable, the desirability is to be explained with reference to the agent's own desires, his future desires and his present desires, but not any desire to do specifically A.[21] Like Nagel, the subjectivist may distinguish motivated and unmotivated desires and then try to formally characterise desirability in terms of unmotivated desires. All this can be held, without accepting the strong, and to my mind implausible, thesis that desire can never be a reason for action. And moreover, the strong thesis can be rejected without putting realism at risk.

Platts' argument for the strong thesis is inadequate, because it involves dubious assumptions. He assumes that something about a desire, like its phenomenology, must be cited to explain the desire and answer the question 'why does that motivate action?' He assumes that in the absence of some feature of some desire to answer this question, a desire cannot be an explanatory reason or value. Moreover, Platts simply assumes that, in the absence of any phenomenological component, the 'only obvious' alternative explanation of why a desire motivates is that the agent believes its object to be desirable independent of desire. This means that a person cannot be motivated by a non-phenomenological desire for A if he does not believe that A is independently desirable. This is surely false, for when I desire to win at cards my desire is non-phenomenological, but I do not believe that my winning is desirable independently of my desires. Furthermore, when Platts says that we must explain why a desire motivates in terms of the subject's belief that its object is desirable independently of his desires, he makes the crucial assumption that the explanation of desire must be external to a person's motivational nature. But we can accept the claim that the explanation of desire will sometimes involve the subject's belief that what he desires is desirable, without accepting that the desirability in question is totally independent of the subject's desires and motivational nature.[22]

It is a common view that desire satisfaction is never a reason for action. The arguments in favour of this view usually support only weaker claims, like the claim that it is not always necessary to desire X in order for X to be good. It is compatible with this claim to believe that getting what you want simply because you want it is valuable, and that desire satisfaction can sometimes be a value. However, believing that desire satisfaction is a value does not commit one to giving it a central place in a theory of well-being and harm. One might hold that desire satisfaction is too trivial a value to be relevant to well-being and harm. Furthermore, believing that desire satisfaction is a value does not commit one to holding the dogma from philosophical psychology in a form which is incompatible with moral realism.

Deprived of its support, the weaknesses of the objective theory are more apparent. As it has been expounded, the theory fails to give any positive account of harm and well-being, because it does not provide any criteria for determining when something is desirable or worthwhile. It merely rejects the desire account. Yet surprisingly, exponents of the objective theory do not go beyond this negative stage. They argue that the desirability of activities and experiences is independent of our desires, and should be explained with reference to certain desirability concepts, standards, or norms, without indicating how disputes about what is desirable are to be settled. Platts says we should explain desires in terms of independent desirability, but gives us no explanation of what 'independent desirability' is and why it should matter to us.

What is a primary good for you might not be for me: the concepts 'harm' and 'well-being' are sensitive to variations in individual natures, and an account of well-being and harm must be able to explain this variation. It is not clear that the objectivist can do this, because according to him what is important for well-being and harm is 'not the fact of wanting but the character of what is wanted'.[23] But if what matters is the character of what is wanted, how are we to explain why what is desirable for one person is not for another? To explain this, we need to focus on the different natures of the two persons, rather than just on the character of what they desire, i.e. X. Merely citing the nature of X cannot help us to explain why X is desirable for one person and not another.[24]

What is worthwhile for an individual is a contingent fact. If we had each had different psychological make-ups, then the kind of things which are worthwhile for us would have been different: it is possible to imagine beings for whom the kinds of activity that are meaningful for us have no value at all. It is a contingent fact that we are not like them. So what is worthwhile for a person is a contingent fact dependent on his nature. Consequently, even if it can be shown that an activity or experience is characterisable with a desirability predicate or norm, it still remains to be shown that the activity suits the nature and character of the person. For instance, high-powered jobs have many desirable characteristics, but this is no recommendation for the person who is not cut out for them, and who is more naturally suited to a quiet and peaceful life. Showing that an activity or experience is characterisable with a desirability concept does not show that it is desirable or worthwhile for a particular individual. We also have to consider the nature of the individual.

Harm consists primarily in the absence of certain primary goods, and an account of harm to P must explain why those primary goods are desirable for P. If X is a primary good for P, then this is because of both the nature of P and the characteristics of X. The desirability of X for P consists of a match or fit between the nature of P and that of X. However, in the final analysis it is P's nature that defines which features of X are relevant to the question of what is to count as a primary good for P rather than the other way round. In other words, we should ask 'What aspects of P's nature determine what is a primary good for P?'[25]

In the absence of any argument for the objective theory, these considerations seem to throw us back into the arms of the desire theory; but we have already rejected that embrace: the familiar problems have not since vanished.

IV

It is usual in discussions of well-being and harm to distinguish between objective and subjective conceptions of well-being.[26] An objective conception provides us with criteria for assessing what is in a person's interests which are independent of his desires and preferences, actual and possible. A subjective conception of well-being is not independent of desires. It is easy to present this distinction as a dichotomy, for either a person's well-being is or is not independent of his desires. But when the distinction betwen objective and subjective conceptions of well-being is presented in these terms, we are faced with a dilemma. This is because both the informed desire account, which is the most promising version of the subjective conception, and the objective account should be rejected. If both the outlined conceptions of well-being and harm are inadequate, this throws doubt on the dichotomy which makes them look exhaustive and incompatible.

The problem stems from treating the idea that well-being and harm is either dependent or independent of desire too loosely. To

escape the dichotomy between objective and subjective conceptions, it is necessary to examine with more care the question of
what it is for a person to have a desire for X. Since the notion of
desiring itself contains a wide range of different psychological
states, it is necessary to examine the range of phenomena which
shelter under the umbrella term 'desire'. In this section, I shall
examine the notion of a desire in the hope that this will help to solve
the apparent dilemma.

The discussion must specify conditions which are necessary in
order for a person to desire X. Special attention ought to be paid to
the notion of the object of desire, that which is wanted. When we
ascribe a desire to a person, we must ascribe a desire with a content,
and this content is provided by the object of the desire. The notion
of an object of desire points in two important directions: first, it
defines desire satisfaction, when this is construed in terms of getting
what you want, or the obtaining of the object of desire, and second,
it provides the most common way of individuating desires. The
notion of the object of desire cannot be defined in terms of what
satisfies the desire, unless we define desire satisfaction in terms
other than the object of desire obtaining. Otherwise the definition
will be circular: we will be defining object in terms of satisfaction
and satisfaction in terms of object. To break out of this circle, we
should try to understand the notion of the object of desire in terms
of the individuation of desires.

The general parameters of this discussion are set by two problems
likely to face anyone trying to specify conditions necessary in order
for a person to desire X. The first problem is how to avoid a tedious
proliferation of desire states. Here it is helpful to be sensitive to the
variety of explanations which can be brought to bear on action. We
ought to recognise that the actions can be habitual and mechanical,
and that actions have a structure, for instance that my action of
forming a particular letter is adequately explained by its being a part
of my action of writing a sentence, without evoking a desire, for
example, to make a cross on a 't'. Clearly, then, we do not have to
postulate a desire behind every action, and this makes it all the more
acute to answer the question 'When is it correct to ascribe a desire to
a person?'

The first problem is due to the fact that not every action is caused
by a desire. Our second problem is due to the fact that not every
desire that a person has causes action. In laying down the conditions

which are necessary in order for A to desire X, we should avoid being too specific. For otherwise, instead of indicating conditions which are necessary for a person to desire X, we shall end up characterising only certain types of desire, and some types of desire may escape our net. For this reason, I shall present these necessary conditions in the form of a disjunction: all types of desire must satisfy at least one of the disjuncts, and some desires will/may satisfy all the disjuncts.

What is it to desire X? It is best to begin by examining the role of desire as an explanatory reason for action, because it is central to the notion of desiring that this can explain intentional action. Anscombe says that the primitive sign of wanting is trying to get.[27] Although this is true, not every desire results in action. To accommodate this point, a person's desiring X can be defined as his being in a state such that 'if it were to occur to him that a certain act of his would tend to bring X about, then his tendency to perform that action would be increased.' Following Brandt,[28] who gives this definition, we should distinguish between effective, occurrent and normal wants. These are not so much different types of desire but rather different kinds of desiring. A person occurrently desires X when he would have an increased disposition to act were he to make the appropriate judgments. A person 'effectively' desires X when he has an occurrent desire for X, and is actually thinking about X. So, having an occurrent desire is more dispositional than effectively desiring and having a normal desire is more dispositional still. A person normally desires X when he often has an occurrent desire for X, even if he does not now have an occurrent desire X. After just finishing a huge steak, I do not have an occurrent desire for meat, although usually I do want meat.

Of these three types of wanting, we should concentrate on effective desires, because these are the least dispositional. By grasping what is involved in 'effectively' desiring X, we can understand the concepts of occurrent and normal desires. According to Brandt's analysis, even when a person 'effectively' desires X, because he actually judges that an action will bring about X, he may still not perform the action. This is because 'effective' desiring is tied to being disposed to act, rather than to action itself. Nevertheless, it is essential to the concept of a desire that desires can function as an explanatory reason for intentional action. Although 'effective' desires need not result in intentional action, it is essential to the concept of a desire that they can do so. I shall argue that the way in which desires do explain intentional action requires some awareness of desire.

In the standard case, desire explains intentional action in conjunction with belief or judgment, by being the agent's own reason for action. When an agent acted intentionally, he did what he did because he wanted to and this was his reason for action: 'intentional actions are distinguished from other conscious voluntary actions in virtue of the agent's state of mind with regard to the results of his action.'[29] In other words, if an agent acts intentionally, then he has a desire as his reason for acting in the way he did. To attribute to an agent a desire as his reason for action requires that he be aware of what answers this desire in the context of the action. It is as if the agent explicitly formulates to himself 'this is what I want and this is the way to get it' – this is the force of saying that his action was intentional. So, if desires are to be the agent's reasons for intentional action, then the subject must be in some way aware of his desire.

The way in which the awareness of desire enters into the explanation of action can be rather oblique, and so we should start with the straightforward case first. In the straightforward case, the origin of an intentional action is the subject's awareness of his desire, and the desire engages with a suitable belief through the awareness. If some awareness condition were not satisfied, the desire and the belief could not be the agent's own reason for action, and the action could not be intentional. In the straightforward case, we may say that the recognition of desire is necessary for the explanation of action to be in terms of the agent's own reasons. A person whose desire for X does not in any way impinge on his awareness cannot recognise what answers his desire, and so, even if he believes that A is necessary for X, this belief will not strike him as relevant or important. If this were the case, neither his belief nor his desire could be called his reason for acting. For example, if I desire to watch television, but I do not recognise that I have this desire, I can be in the same room as a television, and it will never occur to me to turn it on. Although I believe that the television is in front of me, this belief is dead; it has no more relevance to me and what I should do than the belief that Mercury has no moons. Now, if in this situation I were to find myself turning the television on, then according to the standard model, the desire cannot be my reason for doing so. This is because in the standard case, if a desire is a person's reason for action, the subject recognises his desire, and this recognition is essential to the way in which the desire interlocks with a suitable belief to cause action. When a desire engages with a suitable belief via the subject's awareness of his desire, and when this results in intentional action, the desire is the agent's own reason for acting.

This may be misunderstood. That we are non-inferentially aware of our effective desires does not imply that this is due to some special act of introspection. The awareness of desire is more akin to the way in which one knows where one's limbs are without inferring the location from any special sensations. Furthermore, being aware that you want X should not be confused with feeling a desire for X: I know that I want to learn Arabic, but this desire is not associated with special sensations.

So far I have dealt with the straightforward case, where the links between the awareness of desire and the agent's having that desire as a reason for acting intentionally are explicit and above board. However – and this is typical of the pliability of our ordinary concepts – there are deviations from the standard case, so that the awareness point is not readily delineated by a neat formula. The awareness of desire can be a matter of degree; it can be more or less dim, covert and inarticulate; also, it can be sublimated and may not involve awareness of the awareness. We can accept the idea that an unconscious desire is the agent's reason for action and not sever the normal links between desire, belief, and intentional action, by attributing to the subject a subconscious awareness of his desire. We do not have to deny the possibility that an unconscious desire can be a person's reason for action. But, if we are to preserve the normal links between desire, belief and intentional action, and we attribute a desire to a person at a level deeper than everyday consciousness, then we must attribute to him an awareness of the desire at the same level of consciousness.

This is the first deviation from the standard case; the second is that we allow the awareness to be counterfactual. Suppose that I am presented with two cakes and asked to pick one. I am not aware of any preference between them, but I choose the chocolate one. It might be said that I desired the chocolate one and this was my reason for action, on the counterfactual supposition that I would have been aware of my preference had I picked the other cake. Had I chosen the other cake, I might have said in disappointment 'Now I know that I wanted the chocolate cake.' Sometimes we say that an action was done for a reason which can only be formulated after the event. Sometimes, such after-the-event awareness will only be postulated counterfactually, as in the example.

If a person 'effectively' desires X then he judges that some action of his A will tend to bring about X. But also many of our desires, whether they are instrumental or not, depend on beliefs, and especially on beliefs about the desirability and availability of what we desire. For instance, my desire to learn Arabic is dependent on a complex set of beliefs relating to the beauty and usefulness of the language, and the generosity of the people who speak it. My desire to complete my collection of Sumatran butterflies is dependent on my belief that my collection is incomplete. Without these beliefs, I would not have the relevant desires. This is true of occurrent and normal as well as effective desires. Therefore, this dependence of desire on belief should not be confused with the previous point, which concerned the way in which effective desires and judgments combined to cause action. Desires depend on beliefs, whether they bring about action or not, and this dependence has important implications for the phenomenon of wanting. On this dependence hinges the possibility of revising one's desires and preferences by acquiring new information and changing one's beliefs, albeit that some preferences might be stubbornly resistant to such change. This point is obviously vital to the informed preference account of welfare. Furthermore, Marxists are fond of drawing attention to the indefinite expansion of desire in capitalist societies, and these are belief-dependent desires: advertisements cause us to have new beliefs and new desires.

Many cases of wanting can be characterised as acts of choice, and this includes the preference scales used by some Utilitarians, where preference is aptly referred to as preferential choice. How do preference and desire involve an element of choice? Aristotle claims that a distinctive feature of man is his capacity to originate his actions by choice. Clearly, some voluntary actions originate in desire and deliberation on desire. To accommodate this point, we might define desiring in its most effective form as choosing to act in a way that will bring about what we desire, and instead of defining effective desire in terms of being disposed to act, we might define it in terms of being disposed to choose to act: person P 'effectively' desires X when it occurs to him that action A will tend to bring about

X and as a result of this he will have an increased disposition to choose to do A. These moves help to make the links between desire and voluntary action more explicit. However, they do not get to the heart of what is meant by saying that preference is an act of choice. For what is meant by this is not what we can choose how to act, but that desiring itself, whether it results in action or not, is a kind of choice.

Alternatively, we might draw attention to the fact that many of our desires we choose to have, in the sense that they are formed by deliberation and choice and that we can exercise control over them. However, this is not true of all our desires, for typically some desires assail us, come unbidden, and we have very little control over them. Anyhow, this too seems beside the point, which is not whether we can choose our desires, but whether they are acts of choice, and if so, in what sense.

Why is it natural to talk of preferential choice, of rational preferences as rational choices, and of the ranking of preferences as the ranking of choices? How is preferring X to Y choosing X rather than Y, without its necessarily being a choice to bring about X rather than Y? Let us start with an example where the notion of preferential choice is most safely at home. At the end of a show a person is asked to pick out in order of preference the prizes that he would assign, or at the ballot we are asked to pick out in order of preference a candidate. By numbering or pointing in an order, we indicate our preference as if to say 'I choose X, but if I cannot have X, then I shall choose Y . . .' Note the performative element here; this is because in indicating one's preference ranking, one is doing all one can in the context to bring about that which one prefers to obtain. It seems that in at least some versions of the preference theory, one is asked, as it were, to imagine a hypothetical situation where all possible states of affairs are laid out in front of one, like candidates at the end of a show, and where one is asked to choose between them in an order of preference. This analogy highlights that preference here is that something should come about. A person prefers X to Y in the sense that he prefers that X should come about, and in this sense, he chooses X rather than Y. His preference for X is his choice as to what should come about, and need not involve his actually choosing to act in a way that will bring X about. If a person 'effectively' desires X then he chooses that X should come about, and although he may not choose to act in a way to bring X about, he will have a greater disposition to do so. In some cases, 'effectively' desiring X involves an act of choosing X. This isolates the active element in the least dispositional form of desire. This active element explains why, when a person desires X especially strongly, we say that he has fixed his mind upon it, he has decided upon it, or his heart is set on X. . . . In such cases, a person has chosen X and will not be moved from his choice. Of course, desiring need not be so stubborn and wilful. But that it can be illustrates the active element in desire: that 'effectively' desiring involves the making of a choice.

We started this discussion by saying that we require conditions which are necessary for a person to desire X. These conditions must help us to indicate when it is correct to ascribe to a person a desire for X, and in this way avoid a proliferation of postulated desire states. The discussion has yielded the following constraints:

1 If a person 'effectively' desires X, then his desire is potentially his reason for intentional action, because it has engaged with a suitable belief. This requires that the subject be aware in some way that he desires X.

2 If a person desires X then he will have beliefs about the desirability and availability of X, without which he would not desire X.

3 If a person effectively desires X, then he consciously chooses that X should come about.

These three conditions are disjunctively necessary for a person to desire X. If P desires X, then at least one of the disjuncts must be satisfied; some desires will satisfy all three disjuncts. However, it might be argued that some desires satisfy none of the above disjuncts, and to cover this possibility, we should search for a further disjunct which covers the exceptions.

Desires which escape the first condition are those which do not explain action in conjunction with belief by citing the agent's own reason for acting intentionally. With such desires, the subject need not be aware of his desire in order for the desire to explain action. These desires simply drive us, or move us to act, or they form the basis of instinctive reactions. Exceptions to the second condition will be desires which do not depend on beliefs about the desirability and availability of their objects; typically, some impulses which arise from within are like this. Desires which are exempt from the third condition are those which cannot be characterised as acts of choice; perhaps desires which assail us and come unbidden are like this.

It seems plausible to maintain that some desires are not captured by the three disjuncts. The nature of the exceptions highlights a general contrast which is central to any classification to types of wanting. There is what might be called 'a phylogenetic scale of wants'. At one end of the scale there are the more sophisticated desires, which do satisfy at least one of the three disjuncts. These are conscious desires which are potential reasons for action; they are typically formed by deliberation, are themselves acts of choice and are dependent on complex beliefs, and hence on the type of conceptual apparatus which requires language. Because they normally require language, such desires can transcend the behaviourally specific, and the promptings of particular sense stimuli. For this reason, such desires do not necessarily assail us like impulses. At the other end of the scale, there are simple desires which do not depend on belief, judgment, and language. Typically because of this, they are directed towards the behaviourally specific, and are caused by the promptings of sense stimuli, rather than being formed by deliberation and choice. For this reason such desires tend to assail us like impulses, drives and instinctive reactions.

I have presented the contrast between simple and sophisticated desires, the two ends of the phylogenetic scale, in a simplified manner. Nevertheless, a significant point emerges from the contrast: the desires which escape the previous three conditions tend to be those located at the lower end of the scale, and such desires are directed to the particular, i.e. towards a particular plate of food, or object of fear or lust. Thus we can add to the previous conditions, one relating to particularity.

Such an addition is not *ad hoc*. For, of course, very sophisticated desires can have particular objects, and this point seems essential to the nature of desire in general. The notion of what a person wants points towards the world, and it cannot do that without in the end pointing towards a particular piece of it. Suppose that I feel a desire for fun. My desire is not directed towards any particular source of fun but it will become so directed, when it expresses itself in action. Desires are for the particular or they can be made particular. A desire becomes directed towards a particular when it finds expression in action.

IV

INTERESTS: THE ROOTS OF DESIRE

A thing wherein we feel there is some
hidden want

Shelley

In the last chapter we were faced with a dilemma because we had rejected both objective and subjective conceptions of well-being and harm. The dilemma is dependent on our treating the two types of account as exhaustive and incompatible. However, there is an alternative which, as it were, sits mid-way between the purely objective and subjective accounts. In this chapter I shall begin an outline of this middle path, and suggest why it constitutes a more fruitful way of regarding well-being and harm. Harm cannot be understood solely in terms of desire satisfaction as this is usually construed; this is a reason for calling the promised account 'objective'. On the other hand, the account I shall sketch is based on a person's desires, and this is a reason for calling it 'subjective'.

The misleading dichotomy comes from thinking that harm must be construed either in terms of what a person specifically wants, or in terms of the desirability of activities and experiences which is totally independent of our desires. But desirability can be explicated with reference to our desires without being tied to the specific content of what we want. There is an alternative to saying either that well-being must consist in desire satisfaction or desires are completely irrelevant to well-being and harm. To develop this alternative, we require a more complex view of desire and a person's motivational nature. Our understanding of a person's desires and motivational nature is not exhausted by knowing what he wants: there is more to desire than what it is directed towards, or what its object is.

To escape the dilemma, the value of the primary goods we are deprived of when we are harmed must be characterised with reference to a person's desires but not in terms of what he desires. We must say that X is valuable or worthwhile not because a person desires X, but because X serves some other feature of a person's motivational make-up. In this way, harm will not be totally independent of our desires, but neither will it be tied to formal desire satisfaction, or getting what we want.

What aspect of desire is there other than what we desire? Apart from knowing what a person desires, we may also need to know why he desires what he does. But the reasons for desire cannot always be assimilated to the means-end model of explanation. The means-end model is applicable when the desire to be explained is instrumental rather than intrinsic. In this case, we explain the desire by citing the agent's reasons for having this desire, and this involves the citing of another desire: A desires X because he believes that X is a means to Y, and because he desires Y. This model of explanation does not apply to intrinsic or non-instrumental desires. With intrinsic desires, a person has no conscious reason for his desire and expects no instrumental benefit from getting what he wants: he does not desire X because it is a means to the satisfaction of another desire. Suppose I wish to climb a mountain. I have no conscious reason for wanting to do this and so my desire is non-instrumental. Yet there is a reason for my desire, which I may not be able to articulate. The desire, as it were, expresses a need for excitement, to achieve, to pit skills against the risk to life. Such explanations give the reason for a desire because they reveal the motivational nature of the desire, but they do not give the person's own reasons; they are not reasons he consciously has. These reasons may not be acknowledged by the subject, and so such acknowledgment cannot be essential to their existence, nor to the fashion in which they explain.

For the sake of convenience, I shall reserve the term 'interest' for the reasons which lie behind a person's non-instrumental desires. A description which specifies a person's interests indicates the motivational nature of his desires, and in this way it specifies an empirical feature of a person's desires. However, it does not indicate the object of his desires, what it is that he desires. Descriptions which specify a person's interests inform us of why a person desires what he does, but without telling us what he specifically does desire. This suggests that the notion of an interest is quite different from that of a desire, because desires are identified and individuated with reference to their objects, or what it is we desire.

First, I shall draw attention to the intuitive need for a distinction between our interests on the one hand, and our object individuated desires on the other. Secondly, I shall explain the distinction more precisely and argue that the difference is one of kind, that X's being one of our interests is distinct from our desiring X. Thirdly, I shall show why characterising harm and well-being in terms of our interests is significantly different from the desire account of harm and well-being.

It is commonsensical to believe that some distinction ought to be drawn between, on the one hand, our desires and what they are directed towards and, on the other hand, the interests which lie behind our desires. It is also plausible to maintain that these two need not coincide, and that this is relevant to harm and well-being. Unfortunately, thc intuitively obvious sometimes resists the ideal rigours of philosophical precision and does not for that reason disappear, however much we may wish to forget it. In this particular case, ignoring the commonsensical has the disadvantage of distorting reality. It distorts, for instance, the notions of harm and well-being to pretend that these can be characterised without appeal to a theory of human nature and motivation, the kind of theory which investigates the general motivational nature of our desires, the reasons which lie behind our desires. Even when adequate substantial theories of this kind are lacking, it is philosophically necessary to articulate the conceptual frameworks that such substantive theories require. Virtually no current discussion of harm and well-being does this.

The remedy is to provide the formal framework which allows for desires not to be taken at face value, and which allows for some diagnosis and interpretation of desires which transcends merely specifying their objects. Freud, for instance, distinguished between the object and the aim of desire.[1] He took the aims of desires to be certain basic pleasures related to the satisfaction of instinctive drives. However, we do not want to commit ourselves to any substantial view as to what the aims of our desires are. Moreover, Freud's distinction between aim and object of desire is not clear because he characterises the aim of a desire in terms of what satisfies the desire; since the satisfaction of desire can also be defined in terms of the object of desire, this fails to distinguish aim and object. However, what does emerge from Freud's discussion is the need for some distinction between the motivational force of a desire, and what the desire is directed towards, i.e. its object. Such a distinction is required to explain how desire may shift from object to object, and how something, the motivational force, remains constant through such shifts. To maintain such a distinction requires the interpretation of desire and, to some extent, such interpretation is already inherent in everyday practice: we do not always trust a person's desires, as identified by their objects or what he desires, to coincide with his interests. It may take considerable knowledge of a person's character and wide experience of human nature in general, to know how to interpret a person's desires, and to know how to read from these the interests that motivate the desires.

Cases where the reasons for desire (i.e. interests) do not coincide with the object of desire are quite commonplace. For instance, take a man who works hard in order to impress his friends. We might say of such a person that what he really wants is not so much praise but stable affection, but it is easy to mistake this point. We should not say that he desires affection, for the man may actually shun close ties: on the contrary, he desires the kind of praise which comes from hard work and success, even though to his mind, this requires distancing himself from others. However, underlying this desire for success, there is an interest or want for affection. Clearly, this interest will not directly explain his behaviour (of working hard and shunning friendship). The interest does not explain his actions, but it does explain his desire for praise and success, and it is this desire which explains his actions. So, whereas the interest is the reason for desire, the desire is the person's reason for action. The type of explanation in the two cases is different, and this will enable us to pin-point later the differences between interests and desires.

In the above example, there is a difference between what the person desires (praise and success) and what underlies and motivates this desire (his interest, affection), and this difference should not be presented as a contrast between two desires because the person does not desire affection. In this case, the need for a distinction between the person's interest, the reason for his desire, and the desire itself as identified with reference to its object, is obvious. However, this does not obviate the need for the same distinction when it is not so obvious, i.e. when a person's desires and interests do coincide. In the example, success and praise are things the person has chosen, and in this sense he desires them; these are what 'he attaches value to'. Affection and security he has rejected; he is consciously adverse to them, and he does not actively seek them nor is he disposed to. So, if these are constituents of his well-being, this is not through any choice that he has made, and not because he desires them.

The element of choosing is essential to many forms of desiring, including the preference scales used by Utilitarians. Exclusive attention to this type of desire and preference, at the expense of the reasons for desire, creates a false impression of desire. It gives the impression that desires can be understood wholly as atomic acts of choice, whereas, in fact, desires are naturally structured and patterned by their motivating interests. Desires can be understood as acts of choice only within this structure or pattern, which is itself independent of choice. Concentrating on desires as atomic acts of choice creates the false impression that something can be of primary value to a person because of some choice or prescription that he has made. Under the influence of this impression, some philosophers have talked of choosing and creating values in a way that is quite mistaken. These points will be examined later, and I mention them now to illustrate the importance of a desire/interest distinction.

If we conflate a person's desires and their motivating interests then it will appear that almost anything can be a motivating interest. For, in a sense, a person can desire just about anything.[2] So long as he makes the appropriate judgments, a person can desire death, illness, loneliness and unhappiness. A person can desire to be lonely and actively seek to be lonely, when for instance he believes that to do otherwise is a form of weakness which keeps him from God. He might succeed in convincing himself that loneliness is not unpleasant: sadness often feels deep and beautiful. Because, given the right background story, a person can desire anything, it is wrong to appeal to notions like 'what any man desires' in an elucidation of harm and well-being.[3] Although a person can desire anything, it is not the case that anything could be a human interest, and so it is necessary to distinguish a person's desires, which are belief dependent, and his interests, which are belief independent. The view that a person can desire anything is plausible because of the dependence

67

of desire on belief, and because all sorts of crazy beliefs are possible. The corresponding view that almost anything could be a human interest is implausible because our interests are not dependent on belief.[4] For instance, if a person desires to buy a painting, his desire depends on his judgments about the desirability and cost of the painting. On the other hand, if a person has aesthetic interests then he has aesthetically motivated desires, but the fact that he has aesthetically motivated desires is not dependent on any judgment that he makes about the desirability or cost of beautiful things. He may not even realise that he has aesthetic interests, and may not consider or think about the beauty of things.

The evidence for our interests is the way in which they explain desires by naturally structuring them. The motivating source of desire provides a natural, choice-independent grouping and organisation of desire. Thus, it provides an alternative way of individuating desire. Even when a person desires X at time t and Y at time t^1, we may say that this is the same desire. For example, if a person desires an expensive suit at one time and then a large car, we say this is the same desire taking a different shape. Because desires that are individuated in terms of their objects are dependent on belief, as a person acquires new beliefs so what he desires changes, and in this sense, he has different desires. But such change does not amount to transformation, for the motivating source of desire remains constant. The force of the desire shifts from object to object, or put another way, the motivating interests take a different shape according to the pressures of changing belief. If our motivational nature is structured like a web, the outer pattern of desires individuated in terms of their objects change with belief. The central core of the web remains stable and permanent, constituted by motivating interests, which are belief independent. Changes in the central core constitute a transformation in character and nature. As the outer ring of the web is in flux, sense and order can be made of this flux by concentrating upon the relatively stable motivating interests.

It is tiresome to hint at a distinction between desire and interests, without outlining the nature of this distinction. Even if one can indicate the significance and need for such a distinction, one cannot rely too long on the rhetorical effects of phrases like 'real interests'. However, mistrust of such phrases should not lead us to ignore the commonsensical features of motivation that they indicate. Nor should it lead us to think of these terms as value words to be analysed prescriptively. The mistrust should lead us to examine with care the differences between interests and desires.

First, note that other philosophers have felt that object-identified desire is not the only feature of our motivational make-up relevant to the concepts 'harm' and 'well-being'. Scanlon,[5] for instance, gives a very suggestive account of well-being in terms of concerns. After distinguishing objective and subjective accounts of well-being and harm, he argues against a purely subjective desire and preference account. Yet he tries to avoid the rigidity of most objective accounts by trying to characterise well-being in terms of concerns, whose urgency varies with satisfaction over time. Clearly, Scanlon thinks that the notion of a concern is distinct from the concept of a desire, and he also thinks that it is a matter of empirical fact what typical human concerns are. However, he never gives us any criteria for a concern, no clue as to how we should discover what concerns a person has, and, moreover, no way of distinguishing concerns from desires and preferences. This is fatal to his aims, because the subjectivist can argue that the appeal to concerns is a disguised reliance on the notion of a desire. Scanlon obviously intends his view to be distinct from the desire theory of well-being, but he never makes it clear how it is different. It seems that Scanlon is attempting to identify some notion, at least, very similar to that of an interest.

The difference between desires and interests (or more accurately, between desires as identified by their objects, and the reasons for those desires) can be made explicit with an example:

Walking down the street I spot a car and immediately I desire it. This desire is dependent on a complex set of beliefs: judgments I make about the usefulnesss of such a car, its colour, shape, size and beauty: judgments that the car I see is available at a certain price, that I do not already own a car, and that I am unlikely to be given one in the near future . . . After hovering around the car deliberating, I decide to go to the bank and check my balance. Drawing on the discussion from the previous chapter, we can see that the relevant features of the situation are as follows:

1 The dependence of my desire in the context on certain beliefs and judgments about the desirability and availability of the car.
2 The fact that the desire explains my action of going to the

bank by engaging a suitable belief (that I need money) and
forms a part of my reason for going to the bank; this coupling
of the desire and the belief works through my awareness of
my desire.

3 My desiring the car is an act of choice, i.e. I choose that it
should come about that I own the car.

4 The object of my desire is specific and particular.

Because desiring to own a car is a common phenomenon readily
explicable in instrumental terms, we tend not to seek for deeper
non-instrumental explanations of the desire. However, owning a
car can serve non-instrumental interests. To explain the non-
instrumental aspect of the desire, we must show what motivates it.
We must redescribe the desire to make the motivational source
and force of the desire more and more explicit. In effect, we must
subsume the desire under increasingly more general descriptions
so that the interests which motivate the desire become apparent.
These descriptions will show what kind of desire my desire is, and
in this way reveal what it has in common with other superficially
different desires. For instance, my desire can be redescribed in
terms of interests relating to status, domination, admiration.
Other desires may be motivated by similar interests, e.g. the desire
to be well-read, to keep fit.

There are several points to note about interests and the way in
which they explain desire:

1 Unlike the having of desires, the having of interests does not
depend on judgments and beliefs. Having an interest
pertaining to status does not depend on the judgments one
makes about the desirability and availability of status. A
person can be quite unaware that he has an interest pertaining
to status, and may be horrified at the suggestion; yet he has
such an interest, if he has desires which are motivated by
status.[6]

2 In the example, the interest explains my desire to own a car,
but it does not do so in the way that my desire explains my
actions. The desire explains my actions by being a part of my
reason for action, and by engaging a suitable belief. We
explain my desire by showing the interests which are manifest
in the desire: the desire is expressive of those interests. The
interest does not form part of my reason for desiring the car; it

is not a reason I have for the desire but is the reason for the desire. If I had a reason for desiring the car, then the desire would be instrumental. This would be the case, when for instance, I actively and consciously desired status and believed that owning a car was a means to this. In such a case, I would have a reason for desiring to own the car and the desire would be instrumental. But interests explain intrinsic desires non-instrumentally. Because interests explain desires non-instrumentally, they are not the agent's own reason for desire and do not require the engaging of desire with belief; because of this, the explanation of desire does not require recognition of the reasons for the desire. I might be quite unaware of the interests which motivate my desires, although I recognise the desires themselves.

3 Desiring is a form of choosing, but the having of interests is not a form of choice. To have an interest pertaining to affection is not to choose affection. A person has an interest when he has desires motivated by that interest. However, desires motivated by affection need not be directed towards affection. Interests are not a form of choice.

4 In the example, unlike the object of my desire, the reason for desire is non-particular. Even when a desire is not directed towards a particular, it is essential to the nature of desire that it can be made particular. Whilst I start off desiring a car, in the right circumstances I end up desiring a particular car. Being belief-independent, interests cannot be changed in this way and are essentially general and non particular.

In Chapter III, I argued that for A to desire X at least one of four conditions would have to be satisfied. These conditions were offered as necessary conditions of the concept of desiring X or of the concept of a desire as identified with reference to its object. Briefly, these conditions are:[7] either (i) if A has a desire for X, then A will have beliefs about the desirability and the availability of X, or (ii) if A has a desire for X, then this desire can be A's reason for action when the desire engages a suitable belief and this engaging requires that the person be in some way aware of his desire for X, or (iii) if A has a desire for X then he chooses that X should come about, or (iv) if A has a desire for X then X is a particular. If A has a desire for X, then at least one of the conditions (i)-(iv) must be satisfied; sometimes, all four conditions will be met when A desires X, as in, for instance, the example of desiring a car. In this example, it was clear that my desire to own a car satisfied all the conditions (i) to (iv) and moreover, that the interest which motivates this desire satisfies none of the conditions. Because interests satisfy none of the conditions of desire, A can have an interest pertaining to X without actually desiring X. Therefore, we can confidently conclude that interest and desire are distinct concepts, or that descriptions which specify the reasons for a desire are distinct from descriptions which specify the object of a desire. Sometimes, a person's interests and his desires do not coincide, and then the need for the interest/desire distinction is obvious. However, the distinction is still required when a person's interests do coincide with his desires. For this reason, I have examined the notion of a desire and have shown how it differs from that of an interest. This distinction is required primarily to avoid treating desire too simplistically, and to avoid both the purely subjective and objective conceptions of well-being and harm. To understand the significance of the interest/desire distinction for the concept of harm, we must show how characterising harm in terms of our interests is different from characterising it in terms of our desires.

The first and most obvious difference is that of evidence. If we elucidate harm in terms of desire, then to discover what is harmful to a person we must find out what he desires or would desire under certain conditions. One way to do this would be to ask the person, or, at least, to rely on the notion of his potential avowals. If we characterise harm in terms of a person's interests rather than his desires, we cannot have recourse to the same evidence. To know what a person's interests are, we must interpret his desires: we must attend to the way his desires are patterned and organised by their motivational source, rather than simply discovering what it is he desires. In other words, if harm is to be analysed in terms of a person's interests rather than his desires, then the evidence relevant to the nature of harm will be less specific and more complex. It will require the interpretation and diagnosis of desire, and interpretation requires theory. However, it seems correct that some theory of human nature should be required, because it is naive to suppose that we could discover what is constitutive of a person's well-being without a substantive theory of human motivation; as Hollis says: 'there is no dispensing with a model of man.'[8]

Interests: the roots of desire

The most important difference between characterising harm and well-being in terms of interests rather than desires relates to primary value. The significance of the interest/desire distinction is that it provides a way in which something can be of primary value to a person, not because it is desired or would be desired, but because it answers one of his interests. So we have at least two ways in which something can be of primary value: by being the object of a desire, and by answering an interest. An activity can be a primary good, even though a person does not desire to engage in that activity, when the activity answers a person's interests, even when the person is not aware that he has these interests. There are three major differences between the value constituted by being desired and the value constituted by answering an interest.

The desire theorists' premise is that X's having prudential value to P is constituted by X's being the object of some desire of P's. This means that we can only enhance a person's well-being by giving him exactly what he desires. Such desire satisfaction is construed formally: a desire is satisfied if and only if the object of desire obtains, and so it is said that a desire is satisfied in much the same way that a clause in a contract is satisfied: what is specified in the clause or the desire holds. This kind of formal desire satisfaction underpins the informed desire account. But it seems too rigid, because a person's interests can be met without his desires being satisfied. A person may desire just X, but the reason for his desire, the interest manifest in his desire, may be equally well met by Y. When we individuate desires by their motivating interests rather than by their objects, what a person specifically desires seems less important. As one writer put it:[9]

> It isn't as if the desire says 'I want that' and to satisfy it one has to produce just that. Rather it says 'I want something and here's what it should do for me' and then one can search around offering the desire things until something satisfies it.

We may increase a person's well-being without giving him exactly what he desires, but rather by satisfying what lies behind the desire, the interest that motivates it. Therefore, something can be of primary non-moral value to a person without its being the object of a desire.

Secondly, the value of getting what one desires simply because one desires it is intimately related to the recognition of desire. In

73

normal circumstances, if I have a desire to sing, this presents me with a reason for so doing. But now suppose that you are told by a psychologist that you have an unconscious desire to sing, and this desire impinges in no way upon your awareness. Nevertheless you believe the psychologist, and this does not lead you to form a conscious desire to sing, and you do not have any special beliefs about the undesirability of leaving unconscious desires unsatisfied. Thus, if you do have a reason to sing this is simply because you have an unconscious desire to do so. In comparison with the normal case, the reason seems at least very weak. The unconscious desire means nothing to you; it might as well be someone else's desire. It does not relate to any choice you have made, nor to your awareness. Thus the sensible policy, if you believe the psychologist, is to shrug your shoulders and carry on as before, as you would have done had you never been told of this strange fact. Having a desire which does not impinge in any way on one's awareness does not constitute a strong reason for action, even if having a conscious desire does. Thus part of the value of getting what we desire lies in the fact that we are aware of the desire.

This conclusion should not be a surprise, considering both the role of recognition of desire in giving the agent's reason for acting and the close relationship between explanatory and guiding reasons. The value constituted by desire satisfaction requires the recognition of desire, and this mirrors the role of recognition in the explanation of intentional action. However, interests provide the reason for desire, and this does not require the recognition of that reason. The value of X, as constituted by the fact that X answers to a reason for desire, does not require any recognition of that reason. This type of value transcends the recognition requirement, and this provides a point of difference between it and the value of desire satisfaction.

A third difference between the value constituted by being desired and the value constituted by answering an interest is that, whereas some desires are acts of a choice, interests are not acts of choice. Having an interest is not a form of choice and by answering an interest, something can have value for a person whether he recognises it or not, and without his actively choosing or valuing it. On the other hand, the value of desire satisfaction *per se* is in part constituted by the act of choosing. It is as if the person has bestowed what he desires with value by the act of desiring it. By choosing X, X acquires value to the subject. In this context, it becomes natural to talk of 'attaching value to' or 'giving weight or priority to' something. Such value is due to the active element in desire which is the act of choosing; by actively choosing something, it acquires some value for us.

To generalise, if something has value simply because it is desired then this is due to the fact that the subject has chosen just that. Since interests represent the motivational source of our desires, it seems reasonable to argue that, when a desire for X is motivated by an interest, it is more important that the subject should answer the interest than obtain exactly what he desires. This conclusion would be supported by the view that desire satisfaction in itself does not present us with a very strong reason for action – that the simple fact that one has chosen X in itself does not bestow X with much value, albeit that many of the things we desire have value apart from the fact that we desire them. If desiring in itself confers value, then it confers value on that which would otherwise be valueless. When what we desire is otherwise valueless, then it does seem that the value of what is desired simply because it is desired is not very great.

By using the notion of an interest, we can avoid the objective/subjective dilemma described earlier. It should be apparent already that characterising well-being and harm in terms of interests is significantly different from both the objectivist and subjectivist accounts. Let us briefly recap these differences. The objective account says that the primary value of activities and experiences is constituted by the fact that they are truly described with certain desirability predicates, like 'enjoyable', 'exciting', 'beautiful'. This implies that the primary value of activities, etc. is totally independent of our particular human nature. In opposition to this, I have urged that activities are desirable for a person in so far as they answer his interests, and in this sense in so far as they suit his nature. This point does not preclude treating desirability characterisations realistically. For, if people share common interests, then they will tend to group together types of activities which answer those interests, using appropriate desirability predicates, and use those predicates to describe those activities. This means that the stock of desirability concepts will tend to reflect what our common interests are. However, it does not mean that activities which are describable with those predicates are for that reason good. The primary value of activities is constituted by the fact that they answer our individual interests, and is not constituted by the fact that those activities are describable with desirability predicates.

The subjectivist says that the primary value of activities and goods is constituted by the fact that they are desired. Primary goods are the things we desire. In opposition to this viewpoint, I have argued that knowing what we desire does not exhaust our knowledge of desire, and that desires are grouped together in kind according to their motivational nature, the reasons for desire or our interests. In specifying a person's interests, we indicate the point of his desires without specifying the object of his desires. Because primary goods answer our interests, they do not have to be desired. The value of these goods is not constituted by the fact that they are desired, nor by the fact that they would be desired under ideal conditions, but rather by the fact that they answer our interests.

To conclude, the notion of an interest is relevant to the task of explaining the concept of a fundamental need in the following way. The primary goods we are deprived of when we are harmed (by lacking what we need) are good and worthwhile because they answer our interests, and not because they are desired. The notion of an interest defines the range and type of activities and experiences that partly constitute a meaningful, worthwhile life, and it defines the nature of their worth. These types of activities are primary goods and because they are good something which deprives us of them is bad, and harmful.

V

THE NATURAL LIMITS OF CHOICE

> Some unchosen restrictions on choice are
> among the conditions of its possibility.
>
> Nagel

Prudence requires a balance between adapting our environment to suit our nature, and changing ourselves to fit into our environment. In order to improve life, sometimes we must change ourselves rather than the world. For instance, a person may have to lessen his greed, rather than trying to ensure that his greed is regularly satisfied. However, there are limits to the extent to which we can change ourselves, and this point has philosophical significance. One of the aims of this chapter is to indicate the nature of this significance for the concept of harm.

In *Principia Ethica*,[1] Moore asserts that means may be subject to the constraints of natural necessity, but he rejects, without argument, the view that ends too are subject to the constraints of natural necessity. Moore is wrong. Some ends are acquired by chance factors, and are easily given up; other ends are more central and less easily given up. Stamp collecting is an end of the first kind and friendship an end of the second type. In Chapter II, I argued that there are limits to the extent to which we can change ourselves. In this chapter, I shall continue the argument with regard to primary values as defined by our interests. I shall argue that there are natural constraints on what interests we have, and consequently, that there are natural constraints on what can have primary value for us, when this value is defined in terms of our interests. As we shall see at the end of this chapter, this conclusion has important implications for the concepts of harm and fundamental need.

There are three basic positions concerning the limits on primary value and ends which pertain to our well-being and harm. These are:

1 Ultimately, we are free to choose what has primary value for us, and this choice is subject to neither logical nor non-logical constraints.

2 Ultimately, we are not free to choose what has primary value for us, and this is because of the constraints of logical necessity.

3 Ultimately, we are not free to choose what has primary value for us, and this is because of the constraints of non-logical necessity.

I contend that only the third of these positions is defensible. If the broad categories of primary values are defined with reference to our interests, this means that there are natural constraints on what interests we have.

The proposition that we can choose our values is on the face of it false. As Warnock points out, values are almost paradigmatically what we do not choose.[2] However, it does make sense to talk of valuing as a kind of choice. For instance, people value authority more than liberty, and this can be construed as a choice that they either have made or would make. But, although valuing is a form of choice, this is not to say that we choose values, for we should distinguish on the one hand the act of valuing and what we value from on the other hand values and what is valuable.

What is typically meant by saying that we choose our values is to deny that a distinction between what we value and what is valuable can be drawn. What it means to say that we choose our values is that what is of value is ultimately a matter of individual choice, in a way that what is a fact is not a matter of choice. There can be no distinction between what we value or prescribe and what is valuable. If there is no distinction to be drawn between what we value and what is valuable, and if to value or prescribe is a matter of choice, then it is natural to talk of choosing values.

According to prescriptivist theory, evaluative judgments have prescriptive force, which is to say that they entail imperatives. For this reason, an evaluation is neither true nor false and cannot be derived from any statement of fact without evaluative premises. No evaluation can be supported simply by a matter of fact. So those evaluations which can be supported by argument are those which can be derived from premises which must include at least one imperative. For instance, we may support the evaluation 'X is good' with the assertion 'X makes people happy' only given the usually suppressed major premise 'what makes men happy is good'. This evaluative major premise might be rejected, and if it is then the conclusion cannot follow. If one accepts the major premise and should the assertoric minor premise be true, then the conclusion 'X is good' logically follows. In this way, particular evaluations can be supported syllogistically with a further more general evaluative premise. Thus, we are faced either with an infinitive regress of justification or with imperatives which are not supported by argument. Hare calls these unsupported evaluations 'decisions of principle'.[3] The decision of principle underwrites and justifies all the subsidiary imperatives which express more specific acts of evaluation. But how is the decision of principle to be justified? What reason do we have for making one decision of principle rather than another? There can be no reason, it seems, and this is the force of saying that ultimately our values are a matter of choice. The decision of principle cannot be justified by purely factual considerations, but neither can it be justified by a further imperative, for then it would be a decision of principle. There is no sense in which one can know that the decision one has made is correct, for imperatives cannot be true or false.

Thus at root the theory entails that we choose our values. Upon such choices all values and reasons depend, therefore the choice itself is not subject to reasons and cannot be guided by values. It is a choice which is beyond value, but which generates values. The choice of which ultimate principles to accept is not a choice subject to reasons because it is prior to all reasons. Hare says

> We can only ask him (the chooser) to make up his own mind
> which way he ought to live, for in the end everything rests upon
> such a decision of principle.[4]

Two further points should be made about this notion of ultimate choice. First, the whole debate about choosing values has in the past always been confined to the question of moral values, and this tends to cloud the issue. This is because the prescriptivist position is a general theory of value, applicable to prudential as well as moral value. Hare makes this clear in later articles where the notion of desire is analysed in terms of prescriptions, and harm is analysed in terms of the frustration of desire.[5] If the prescriptivist analysis of value also applies to prudential value then the indeterminacy of value which the theory entails will also infect prudence. In other words, prudential values will all ultimately be based on a choice beyond reasons, a decision of principle. There are no constraints on such a decision: a person could decide to prescribe his own pain and unhappiness, could decide to be against human companionship, against a life containing humour, variety, intellectual pursuits, etc . . . According to such decisions, what constitutes a person's welfare and well-being will change, but there can be no reasons for deciding one way and not the other.

The fact that the indeterminacy of value applies to prudential considerations means that the prescriptivist cannot appeal decisively to such considerations to alleviate the indeterminacy in the moral case. Hare seems to make such an appeal when he talks about 'the price of fanaticism',[6] as if there were an objective price which had to be paid for prescribing fanatically. But, of course, the fanatic is free to make his own self-addressed prescriptions, and hence his own interests fanatical too.

The second point about ultimate choice is that it is incorrect to suggest that this constitutes a kind of freedom, and to suggest that to reject the grounding of evaluations upon ultimate choices is to deny to man a kind of freedom. Hare says 'we are free to form our own opinions about moral questions.'[7] This can be taken in many ways. Of course we are free to form our own opinions about any questions, but this does not require the postulation of ultimate choices. We are free to form our own beliefs, but this does not make those beliefs true. What Hare means is that we are free to choose what has value. This freedom amounts to the choice being groundless, not subject to reasons, immune from objective criticism. This is not what we normally mean by 'freedom'; usually we say that a choice is free when the chooser is not under threat, or is not driven to opt for one alternative by the pressure of internal or external forces. We can freely choose the least desirable of several options, although what is the least desirable is not a matter for choice.

The points raised about ultimate choice do not tell conclusively against the main body of prescriptivist doctrine, against for instance the view that evaluations are prescriptions which are neither true nor false and which cannot be entailed by an assertion of fact. Rather they reveal what is implausible about the view that we are free to choose our values, that values are adopted. However, later I shall argue against the main features of prescriptivism, and thereby commit myself to the view that statements about what we have some reason to do and what is valuable and worthwhile are either true or false. The issue of whether prudential value judgments are descriptions or not is independent of the issue of choice. Hare could have said that some prescriptions we make by virtue of our nature and that they are inescapable, although this would require some revision of the notion of prescription. Conversely, the descriptivist could hold that to make a statement about what has primary prudential value is to make an assertion about a person's optional and alterable desires.

However, it seems that what is valuable in life, what is worthwhile, is subject to two important conditions. First, what counts substantively as valuable is logically contingent. It is a contingent fact about us that we have, for instance, aesthetically motivated desires at all, and it is because of this fact that the wide range of aesthetic desirability concepts have application in characterising what is worthwhile and valuable to us. Similarly, it is a contingent fact that we are socially motivated creatures. A whole range of desirable and worthwhile activities and experiences that we are deprived of when we are harmed are contingently desirable. They count as desirable for us because of complex features of our motivational and emotional make-up, and this make-up is a contingent fact. For this reason it is possible to imagine beings quite different from us for whom friendship, the appreciation of beauty, fun, humour, variety, mean nothing at all. This is because they lack the relevant features of motivation, because their nature is deeply different from ours. If we can imagine persons, whether human or not, whose nature does not include any aesthetically motivated desires at all, and for whom there are no aesthetic deprivations, then this suggests that it is by virtue of contingent features of our make-up that aesthetic considerations count towards our well-being and harm. In other words, such primary prudential values are not fixed logically.

One reason why it might be thought that primary prudential

values are fixed logically is as follows. In opposition to Hare, it might be argued that primary desirability concepts cannot be split into a neutral factual element and an evaluative component, and that this is because there is no neutral description which will be able to denote all and only those states of affairs denoted by the desirability concept or predicate.[8] For instance, we cannot give a purely neutral description of what is common to all beautiful things and, therefore, the concept of beauty cannot be separated into two elements, one descriptive and neutral, and the other evaluative. This seems to entail that anything describable with a desirability predicate must have primary value and that primary prudential values are fixed logically. However, it does not. The non-disentanglement thesis, the view that desirability characterisations cannot be split into two components, does not show that primary prudential values are fixed logically. This is because the thesis concerns our ability to use and understand concepts, rather than the question of how adeptly those concepts characterise what is basically good for us. At least, the thesis shows that if one is able to use and understand certain desirability concepts, then one must be able to see the point of the classifications which employ those concepts. However, this does not mean that those concepts must indicate something desirable for the individual: a natural hermit may be able to understand the concept of friendship, and understand that friendship is desirable for most people, without it being desirable for him. At most, the thesis shows that a person will be able to understand a desirability concept only if things which come under that concept have some weight or value for him. But this only shows that if our interests and motivational nature were different then our concepts would be different too. It does not show that primary prudential values are fixed logically.[9] Consequently, even if the non-disentanglement thesis is true, our main point remains unscathed. Our main point was that primary values depend upon contingent features of our make-up, namely our interests, and that therefore statements like 'friendship is a primary good for human persons' are logically contingent truths.

Note that this point concerns primary prudential values, and that it is quite compatible with this point to maintain some other statements about what is desirable and undesirable are analytic. For instance, harm is necessarily bad, and this is because it consists of the deprivation of primary goods, even though these primary goods are contingently desirable or valuable. Statements like 'harm is bad' are analytic, but they do not give us any substantive information about what has primary prudential value for individuals or groups of individuals. Therefore, we should distinguish between primary values, on the one hand, e.g. privacy, friendship, beauty, fun, and humour, and secondary values, on the other, e.g. health, well-being, happiness.

If primary values are logically contingent because they depend upon our nature, then this indicates a second condition to which primary prudential values are subject. This is that, in general, what counts as a substantive primary good is not a matter over which we have much choice. Primary values are relatively non-plastic, and therefore they depend upon relatively inescapable features of our nature. In this respect, there are natural constraints and limits to the extent to which we can change ourselves, and hence limits on the extent to which such change can be a practical option in the search for a better life. There are natural limits to the extent to which we can adapt ourselves and our ends and interests to fit into our environment for the sake of a better life.

Given this point, the distinction between object individuated desires and the interests which explain and motivate those desires, acquires a new significance. First, the distinction allows us to say that a person need not desire X in order for X to be primary value for him. This is because object-individuated desires do not form the only feature of our motivational make-up relevant to well-being and harm. Secondly, the interest/desire distinction allows us to maintain with more plausibility the claim that certain features of that make-up are inescapable. Desires individuated and identified by their objects usually are alterable; it it not clear that we have any desires which we cannot escape. But, although we can exercise control over what we desire, we can exercise much less control over the motivational nature and the structure of our desires. Therefore, the distinction between interests and desires is important for the claim that primary values are relatively inescapable because they are subject to the constraints of natural necessity.

In his article on neutrality in social and political science, Charles Taylor asks questions about social class conflict. He asks whether class tension is an eradicable blot on social harmony or whether it is ineradicable and ever-present, varying only in its forms. If the second is true, then we may never approach the ideal of classless society, and this ideal passes from the realm of normative political discourse to the domain of Utopian fiction. If the struggle between rich and poor is inescapable and can only take different forms, then it is irrational to try and achieve the classless society. Taylor says:

> If we rule out the transformation to a classless society then we are left with the choice between different kinds of conflict.[10]

What the discussion shows is how inescapability can cut across and transform the nature of normative political debate, and how it can establish a new framework for such a debate. I suggest that in rather a similar way, inescapability is an important element in practical reasoning about the rationality of those primary goods which govern our well-being and harm.

If certain general types of activity are inescapably valuable then this is because the interests which define those goods are themselves inescapable. The relative inescapability of interests and hence of primary goods emerges as a vital feature of prudential reasoning, because of its relation to the concept of the given. Any piece of practical reasoning requires that some ends of primary values be treated as given or be taken for granted. These given ends or goods constitute the starting point of deliberation and determine what is relevant to the deliberation. Without a given, reasoning cannot begin; it has no criteria of relevance and no means of selection. Arguably this has a parallel in theoretical reasoning and observation. As Popper maintains,[11] scientists do not simply observe, but come to observation with theoretical problems which direct their inquiry and determine what is relevant to that inquiry. At deeper level, experience requires a framework of beliefs and concepts which determine our classifications and direct our attention. What is similar and dissimilar depends on the concepts which we bring to experience. Just as experience may require a framework of beliefs and concepts, and observation requires a point or purpose for selection, so practical reasoning requires that some ends or primary goods be treated as given.

What we treat as given need not be fully determinate ends or specific and particular primary goods. It can be general types of goods and vaguely defined ends. Therefore, the task of reasoning is not simply to find the appropriate and most efficient means to those ends. On the contrary, much reasoning is still concerned with ends, with how best to translate these vague given ends into more specific ends, like plans of action, in a particular context. The view that practical reasoning requires a given does not imply the thesis that reasoning is solely concerned with means and never with ends. Practical reasoning requires that some ends be treated as given. The relative inescapability of interests partly determines which ends or primary goods may be treated as given. This is because the more inescapable an interest is, the more redundant it becomes to ask whether we ought to have that interest and, at the limit, we neither ought nor ought not to have an interest which is inescapable. Thus, we are completely justified in treating ends or primary goods defined by such interests as given, and, indeed, we are obliged to do so. Because of this, inescapable ends can form the ultimate resting place for a certain type of prudential justification, a given bed-rock. Therefore, the terminal point of justification does not have to be reasonless and groundless choice, like decisions of principle, nor does it have to be logically fixed values. If it is a brute inescapable fact about us that we have certain interests, then the primary goods determined by those interests are to be regarded as given.[12]

In conclusion, what has primary value for a person is not a matter of free choice, but neither are primary values fixed logically. These values are subject to the constraints of natural necessity, or they are determined by the kind of creatures we are and, in particular, what inescapable interests we have. An interest is inescapable if there is little or nothing that can be done by a person to change the fact that he has desires motivated by that interest. The claim that we have a basic framework of inescapable interests does not mean that all interests are inalterable. This is a matter of degree. However, if an interest is escapable or is easily altered, then it is appropriate to ask whether, in the long run, it might be the case that the subject ought to alter his interest. Prudence can require us to change ourselves, and thereby what has primary value for us. The significance of inescapable interests is that they set limits to how radically and deeply we can change ourselves, and that they determine ends which must be taken as given in prudential deliberation. It is in relation to this given multiplicity of goods that we can assess whether we ought to change the more optional sides of our nature. For example, if man can purge himself of aggressive interests, but there are ways of meeting these interests which do not disturb our individual well-being, for instance, by ruining our relationships, then the subject himself is not worse off for having aggressive interests, and thus prudence does not require him to alter this aspect of his nature. In this way, it is possible to include the more optional and plastic aspects of our nature, as well as the inescapable, in our conception of the range of goods relevant to well-being and harm. In other words, our conception of primary goods does not have to be restricted to our inescapable interests. It can include more optional interests, so long as prudence does not require us to change these.

Thus, starting from inescapable interests, we can build a more full-bodied picture of the types of primary goods relevant to harm and well-being. We can use this more full-bodied picture to assess the prudential rationality of particular plans of action in context. This schematic picture of deliberation is required if we are to avoid both the position that we are ultimately free to choose what has value for us and the view that values are determined by logical necessity.

Natural necessity restricts choice and thereby can be a determinant of primary value. This view is preferable to both the position that we have unrestricted choice of primary value, and to the view that primary values are fixed logically. However, the argument so far does not show that it is a requirement of prudential rationality that some ends and interests are inescapable. There is a relatively plausible argument for this stronger conclusion, which I shall sketch briefly. The argument runs as follows: prudential rationality requires that some ends be regarded as given, and we can be justified in treating an end as given only with reference to inescapable interests. We cannot be justified in treating an end as a given with reference to optional interests alone, because with regard to optional interests, it is appropriate to ask 'Ought the subject to have the interest?' If justification must have a terminus and cannot regress indefinitely, then the question 'Ought the subject to have the interest?' cannot repeat itself indefinitely. However, the only way we stop it arising is appeal to an inescapable interest.

The key point in this argument is the claim that justification cannot terminate with the citing of an optional, escapable interest because it is appropriate to ask of such an interest whether the subject ought to have the interest. Suppose the subject ought not to have the interest, then the interest cannot serve as a given in justification. *Ex hypothesi*, the subject's well-being is better served if he purged himself of the interest rather than trying to answer it, and, therefore, such an interest cannot be cited as a given in justification; one cannot justify by citing the unjustified. On the other hand, if the subject ought to have the interest, then this must be because of its relation to other interests, i.e. the types of activity which typically answer this interest are not incompatible with his other interests. If these other interests are themselves escapable or optional, then the question arises with respect to them: 'Ought the subject to have the interest?' The argument then repeats itself at this deeper level, and will continue to do so unless there is a point at which the relative inescapability of an interest justifies us in saying that the question of whether the subject ought to have the interest does not arise. In other words, there will be an infinite regress in justification which can only be halted by an inescapable interest.

Now, it might be claimed against the above argument that justification stops when we cite a desirability characterisation and that the notion of an inescapable interest is therefore not required. In answer to the question 'Why is it good to do A?', we reply 'Because it is amusing' or 'Because doing A will lead you to beautiful countryside'. I deny that justification terminates with the citing of a desirability predicate. First, the citing of a desirability predicate does not show even that an action described with such a predicate is a primary good for an individual. To show that an action is of primary value for a person, we must show that it answers one of his interests. Typically, though, our desirability concepts will reflect our interests, because such concepts are supposed to pick out the desirable features of actions and experiences. But this does not mean that the primary value of actions actually consists in those actions being describable with a desirability predicate, because desirability predicates succeed in picking out the desirable features of actions and experiences only in so far as they pick out what answers our interests. Secondly, in the long term, even if an action or experience does meet a person's interests, this may not mean it is of given primary value. This is because it might be the case that the subject ought to have different interests. To meet this doubt, ultimately, we must appeal to the person's inescapable interests. Therefore, justification does not terminate with the citing of a desirability predicate. It appears to, because in citing such a predicate, we assume a shared human nature, which includes common deep interests – we assume a shared form of life.

It may seem that this chapter has been a digression from the main aim of explaining the concept of a fundamental need. This impression is mistaken for three reasons. First, the concept of an interest must form an integral part of the concept of a fundamental need, because our interests determine in general terms what types of activities and experiences we are deprived of when we are harmed. We require the notion of an interest to explain what harm is, and we require the notion of harm to explain what a fundamental need is. The concept of an interest demonstrates in what sense our well-being consists of living in accordance with our nature, rather than consisting of getting what we desire. The significance of inescapable interests is that these define in what way we must treat this nature as given. They provide a certain starting-point for deliberation and a certain fixedness in what is to count as good or bad for a person.

Secondly, this fixedness is required by the concept of a fundamental need. The thesis that fundamental needs are inescapable requires that our interests are unalterable. For, if fundamental needs are inescapable, so too must be the harm consequent on lacking what we need; and this means that interests must be inescapable, because these define what types of activity we are deprived of when we are harmed. If we could easily alter our interests, then we could change what harm is and thereby escape our needs. A theory of harm must be able to accommodate the claim that fundamental needs are inescapable. This is a problem for desire-based views of harm. According to such a view, the primary goods we are deprived of when we are harmed are valuable because they are desired. Therefore, on such a view, if desires are alterable and revisable, then harm and needs can be escaped. For example, health is usually considered a need because ill-health deprives a person of so much. But, if a desire-based theory of harm were true, and if a person could alter his desires so that he no longer desired any of the things which ill-health deprives him of, then health could not be considered a need. To preserve common-sense and the thesis that fundamental needs are inescapable, it must be admitted that we have limited control over the nature of harm and what has primary value for us, and thus limited control over our interests.

Thirdly, we should not confuse interests and needs. Interests define a certain type of primary value, and thus play a prominent part in theories of well-being, welfare and harm. On the other hand, objects of need have secondary value. They are inescapably necessary to avoid harm. The value of needed things should be explained in relation to harm and, thus, interests. Interests define what harm

88

consists of; needs are necessary to avoid that harm. For this reason, we should oppose a theory of welfare and harm which attempts to explain these concepts in terms of 'need'.[13] Because 'need' is to be explained in terms of 'harm', we require an elucidation of 'harm' which does not involve the concept of a need. Harm does not consist in the frustration of needs, although the frustration of needs will inevitably cause harm.

VI

RELATIVITY

Sooner or later everything runs into
its opposite.

Jung

Not every 'need' statement indicates the existence of a need, let alone a fundamental need. Jupiter needs a certain minimum momentum to stay in orbit round the Sun, but we cannot conclude from this that Jupiter has needs. Furthermore, not every need that a person has is fundamental; some needs are purely instrumental. A need is purely instrumental when it pertains to the necessary conditions for a person to complete his goals, projects, and plans, and when the person is not seriously harmed by being unable to complete those goals, etc. So, whilst we may agree that a person needs a hammer to complete his job, we may refuse to accept that he *needs* to complete his job, if he will not be seriously harmed if he gives it up (indeed, it may be beneficial for him to do so). A person has a fundamental need for X if he must be inescapably and seriously harmed so long as he lacks X. The difference between fundamental and instrumental needs rests on the fact that harm does not consist in the frustration of desire.[1] To lack what one desires does not in itself constitute harm, because harm is interest-rather than desire-based. Consequently, fundamental needs are not necessary for the satisfaction of desire.

To characterise what a fundamental need is, we must explain what serious harm is. To say that something harms a person is to say something about the effects of that thing on the person or his life and well-being. The conclusions we have reached about harm are:

1 Harm is the deprivation of types of goods, and not the deprivation of particular goods, like meeting a friend at a particular time.[2]
2 These types are defined with reference to a person's interests rather than his desires.[3] Harm does not consist in the failure to get what one desires.
3 Harm may involve disliked states of mind, and, although it need not, it is all the more serious if it does, all other things being equal.[4]

The account of harm so far is still rudimentary, because it is still unclear how harm differs from the absence of an unneeded benefit, and it is also unclear what type of harm generates needs. Later in this chapter I shall clarify these points and distinguish needs, benefits, goods and luxuries. Despite the remaining unclarities, the analysis so far enables us to characterise what is distinctive and special about the concept of a fundamental need. Briefly, this is the way in which use of the concept exploits the notion of necessity. The best way to explain this is by examining the way in which the concept functions in its paradigm instances like the need for food and water. By grasping the working of the concept in these standard and often-cited cases, we shall see how the concept legitimately extends beyond the bounds of survival needs to more contentious cases.

Earlier in Chapter I we noted a metaphorical interplay between notions of natural and practical necessity, between natural modals and terms which express strong reasons for action. This type of interplay is an essential feature of the concept of a fundamental need, because 'I need X' carries the implication that X is both a necessary condition and is practically necessary or indispensable. These two implications are combined because what one needs is inescapably necessary for something of importance to the subject of the need. A needed object is indispensable because it is an inescapable necessary condition of the subject's not suffering serious harm. Thus, seriousness is part of the logic of 'need'. There is evidence for this. First, there is the metaphorical interplay mentioned earlier: given the general existence of such interplay, we should expect it to function in the specific case of 'need'. Secondly, statements like 'I need X but that is not important' are logically odd. Thirdly, the claim 'I need X' is much stronger than the claim 'I desire X'. Fourthly, needs and luxuries stand as contraries. These are reasons for thinking that the phrase 'fundamental need' refers to something which it is seriously damaging to lack. Nothing trivial can count as a fundamental need, even though something can be needed to complete a trivial task.[5]

The sentence 'fundamental needs are practically necessary' means that in most circumstances a person has a conclusive reason to seek what he needs. This does not mean that needs cannot be overridden. They can be overridden by yet more serious needs, and a person may have a good reason to sacrifice his health or life for some cause, for example. Fundamental needs are practically necessary because they present a person with only two options: necessarily and inescapably, one must either obtain what one needs, or else suffer some serious and otherwise irreversible harm. One must either eat or die. The logic of need restricts our choice to two such alternatives and, because the reasons against one of these alternatives is so strong, there is point and force in saying that we must have what we need. It is as if we had only one course of action available to us, as if we were literally forced to seek what we need. In this way, the potency of fundamental need claims is to be explained by the special combination of necessity, inescapability and seriousness.[6]

So explained, the paradigm instances of need place an obviously strong claim on their subject. However, true need claims of this kind are rare. Taken in its paradigm form, the concept has a restricted application, and this is why the same standard examples of fundamental needs are so often repeated. The rhetorical force of unqualified 'need' claims is substantiated and justified when, no matter what, the subject must suffer serious harm so long as he lacks what he needs. This suggests that we ought to use such 'need' claims carefully and conservatively to remain faithful to the logic of the concept. However, this conceptual demand is vague, and the concept of a fundamental need can be extended beyond its paradigm instances and given a wider application by being weakened. For instance, we can weaken the demand that the harm consequent on lacking what one needs be serious, and by interpreting this demand more liberally, we can widen the application of the concept of a fundamental need.

This weakening is possible because the notion of serious harm is vague. It is vague in two very similar respects. First, what counts as *serious* harm is vague. Even if it is a clear-cut matter of fact how serious one harm is in comparison to other harms, it is still a matter of convention and context how appropriate the term 'serious' is to any instance of harm. What is context-dependent and vague is not the comparative seriousness of particular instances of harm, but whether we call a harm 'serious' or not, like whether we call a stretch of water 'deep'. This means that once we have settled the conceptual question 'What constitutes the fact that one harm is more serious than another?' and the substantive question 'Is this instance of harm more serious than these?', it is a relatively unimportant and mostly verbal question whether we call a particular instance of harm 'serious' or not.

Secondly, in a very similar way, what counts as harm as opposed to non-benefit can also be vague and context-dependent. However, this point depends on what one means by 'harm', for there are two ways of explaining the difference between harm and non-benefit.[7] First, a person is harmed when the quality of his life actually falls, however high it was to begin with, and a person is benefited whenever the quality of his life actually rises. According to this explanation, the distinction between being harmed and failing to secure a benefit is clear-cut. However, it is obvious that the concept of a need does not pertain to this type of harm. For, if a person has never had what he needs, he is still harmed, even though the quality of his life has not actually fallen. Need is tied to the absence of certain primary goods rather than to their loss, and so, to characterise 'need' in terms of 'harm', we should explain harm in the following way: a person is harmed whenever this level of well-being is below a certain level or norm, even if it has not actually fallen. Given this explanation of harm, an unneeded benefit is something which benefits us, but the loss of which does not positively harm us, even though it does cause us to be worse off. For example, my daily exercises benefit me, but the loss of this routine does not cause me harm, even though it does cause me to be worse off than before. This loss does not harm me, because it does not make me positively ill, although it does make me less healthy.[8]

The distinction between this second type of harm and non-benefit can be vague in much the same way that the distinction between serious and non-serious harm is vague. It is not fixed once and for all below what level a person's well-being has to be in order for him to be harmed. It is not fixed how well a person's interests have to be met for him to attain the norm of well-being, to be or fall below which constitutes harm. However, two people can fix this level differently without this entailing any conceptual or substantive differences in their beliefs about harm and well-being. It is as if two people agreed on the shape and co-ordinates of a probability curve and were prepared to draw the level of significance differently. As before, no substantive question of comparative priority rests upon where one draws the norm of well-being, and in this sense, saying that the boundary between harm and non-benefit is not fixed is like saying that the borderline between deep and shallow is vague.

The borderline between harm and non-benefit is vague because harm and well-being are defined primarily in terms of interests, and it is a matter of degree how well a person's interests are being answered. However, there are limits to this vagueness, and this is because of the role that mental states play in a theory of well-being and harm. Positive well-being and benefit typically involve positive mental-states, like feeling useful and secure.[9] On the other hand, harm and need typically involve bad and disliked states of mind. To this extent, the distinction between harm and non-benefit is one of kind rather than degree.

The concept of a fundamental need inherits from the notion of serious harm the two types of vagueness we have discussed. However, no substantive issue of comparative priority hangs on these purely verbal questions about the use of 'serious harm' and 'need'. Therefore, it is a misconception to think that there is a fixed boundary between needs and unneeded benefits, and that where we draw this boundary on any occasion involves an important practical decision. No practical conclusion follows from where we draw such a line and thus, when drawing this line involves stipulation, no practical conclusion rests on stipulation.[10] Of course, there are paradigm instances of need which involve harm which is incontestably serious, and instances of benefits which are incontestably trivial; but in between these two extremes, the boundaries are vague. Since, 'need' pertains to serious harm, and there is no simple context-independent answer to the question 'How bad does harm have to be to merit being called "serious"?', there is no simple answer to the question 'What do we need?' For this reason, it is pointless to try to list human needs once and for all. Furthermore, it is a myth to believe that answers like 'How much education does a person need?' are going to settle questions of priority. We do not settle substantative questions of comparative priority by deciding how and when to use 'need'.

Need is vague, but it is not therefore relative. The view that different societies may typically place a different premium on the terms 'serious harm' and 'need' should be distinguished from various other theses.

1 The vagueness which infects the concept of a need, because of its links with serious harm, should be distinguished from the type of relativity entailed by linking 'need' to the minimum for a decent sort of life. Benn and Peters[11] suggest that statements of basic need involve the concept of a bare minimum for a decent life, and that this varies according to time and place. They suggest that basic fundamental needs are a function of the general standards of living in a community. They say:

> Basic needs are related to norms set by conditions already widely enjoyed. They are needs for precisely those things that most people have got.[12]

This statement clearly implies that if most people have not got X, then X cannot be a need, even when without X they must die. If most members of a community are starving, then they cannot be said to need food. This means that, whereas Americans can be said to need food, people from Bangladesh cannot. Furthermore, if most members of the world community are starving, then no person can be said to need food. Also, by linking need to what is normal in a society, Benn and Peters imply that as standards of living rise, so people's needs increase, and conversely, as standards drop, needs decrease. In other words, people in poorer societies need less than those in rich societies. Common sense tells us that the rich and the poor have similar and equal needs, and that the difference between them is that the poor lack more of what they need than the rich. The point is not that the rich need more than the poor, but that what in poorer societies may be considered a mere benefit, the rich consider a need. But then, what the poor consider a need, the rich must consider a serious need. If richer societies have higher standards and place less premium on the term 'need', then they will have to apply those higher standards to themselves and the poor alike. If we place less premium on the term 'need', we will have to resort more often to the rhetorical effects of phrases like, 'really need', 'truly need' and 'seriously need' to describe what could be described with just 'need'. That is the price of weakening our usage of 'need'.

2 The claim that 'need' is vague, and can be used more or less weakly, is quite distinct from the claim that needs are relative to the minimum standard of living acceptable in a society.[13] Given that the minimum standard of living acceptable in a society rises as wealth

increases, this latter claim entails that people in richer societies need more than those in poorer societies. The claim that I am making does not at all involve the idea of what is or is not acceptable in a society. And for this reason, I think that it is possible to criticise the minimum standard of living which is acceptable in a society for being too low and for failing to cater for people's needs.

3 The thesis that 'need' is vague concerns the borderline between the concepts of a need and a mere benefit. Both needs and benefits involve the notion of well-being as defined with reference to a person's interests. Therefore, we should distinguish both needs and benefits from things which are good but which do not pertain to our well-being. Something can be nice, enjoyable, useful, or desired without enhancing our well-being. In particular, we should not confuse the need/luxury distinction with the need/benefit distinction. A luxury item is something enjoyable, which is neither beneficial nor useful. Whereas needs are indispensable, luxuries are by definition superfluous. The need/luxury distinction is one of kind, even though the need/benefit distinction is sometimes one of degree. Therefore, nothing said so far entails that yesterday's luxuries have become today's necessities.[14] Furthermore, even though the boundary between need and benefit is sometimes vague, it is compatible with this to maintain that lacking what one needs is worse than failing to acquire an unneeded benefit.[15] Intuitively, the three categories need, benefit, and luxury are placed in that order of comparative seriousness, and nothing argued for here contradicts this claim.

4 The claim that to be harmed is to be or fall below a certain norm of well-being is quite distinct from the view that the criteria for harm are social norms, rather than individual interests or desires. According to this latter view, the primary goods we are deprived of when we are harmed are valuable, not because they are desired, nor because they meet our interests, but because they answer certain social norms. In this context, a social norm is a desirability concept which is in common use in a society, and, therefore, something answers social norms when it is describable with certain desirability-characterisations.[16] In other words, the view that the criteria for harm are social norms is equivalent to the objectivist view of harm, which was rejected in Chapters III and IV in favour of an interest-based account of harm.[17]

5 The claim that the concept of harm is vague is also distinct from

the thesis that what counts as harm depends on the subject's conception of human well-being. In opposition to the view that harm is relative to a person's conception of well-being, I contend that what counts as harm depends on a person's interests, and that what interests a person has does not primarily depend on his conception of or beliefs about the good life.[18] Of course, people do have varying conceptions of the good life, but this does not mean that well-being of a person should be judged in terms of his conception, nor in terms of his desires which arise out of that conception.[19] If either a person's well-being were constituted by the satisfaction of his desires which depended on his conception of human well-being, or if we assessed a person's well-being according to his own conception of what that well-being consists of, then it would be impossible to say that his conception was mistaken. If, on the other hand, we judged a person's well-being with reference to his interests, then it is possible to say that his conception of the good life is mistaken. It would be mistaken if such a life failed to answer his interests. It is compatible with this non-relativist view of harm to maintain that people in different societies will tend to have different interests because of variations in their upbringing. It is also compatible to maintain that a person can be harmed because of his conception of the good life: the belief that I have been harmed can itself cause me to be harmed even if that belief is false. For instance, if, according to my own conception of well-being, my life is stunted. then this may cause me to feel depressed and lose confidence and thus actually cause my life to become stunted. But the view that a person's conception of the good life can cause him to be harmed should be distinguished from the claim that what actually constitutes harm depends on a person's conception of the good life.

The aim of the discussions in points 1 to 5 is to distinguish the thesis that the concept of a need is vague from other superficially similar claims. So far it has been argued that the concept of a need is vague because of its links with the notion 'serious harm'. However, the concept of a fundamental need is vague in other ways too. In Chapters II and IV it was argued that the concept of a need involved the idea of relative inescapability. The demand that fundamental needs be inescapable can be construed more or less weakly: we cannot escape our fundamental needs, or more weakly, we cannot easily escape them, or the only way we can escape them must be in some way discountable.

VII

NEEDS AND DESIRES

Desire may be capricious; need always claims
to be taken seriously.

K. Minogue

I

Much of the interest invested in the concept of a need in political
and educational theory is because of the contrast between needs
and desires. The rhetorical force of 'need' claims suggests that
needs are more important than desires. If needs do have rational
priority over desires, then some support is lent to those educational
and social policies and individual projects which aim to meet needs
rather than desires, and perhaps also to those theories which
underpin such policies. For example, Christian Bay argues that the
aim of a political system is to satisfy human needs.[1] He criticises
institutions which fail in this purpose by promoting minority desires
at the expense of majority needs. Bay assumes that needs do have
rational priority over desires, but never defends this assumption.

My aim is not to consider the multifarious issues that would help,
refute or support such wide political claims. It is rather to fill a
particular lacuna in the current philosophical literature by discuss-
ing the thesis that needs have rational priority over desires, and by
examining the differences between needs and desires.[2]

One can desire what one does not need and one can need what
one does not desire. Therefore, 'need' and 'desire' are distinct

concepts: 'A desires X' and 'A needs X' do not entail each other. The major differences between the two concepts are as follows.

1 It is logically impossible for a person to lack what he needs without being seriously harmed. On the other hand, it is possible for a person to lack what he desires without being harmed. It is not a part of the concept of a desire that a person should be harmed when he lacks what he desires. Of course, we cannot conclude from this purely modal difference between 'need' and 'desire' that a person will not be harmed when he lacks what he desires. However, a person can suffer harm when he lacks what he desires, without it being the case that he needs what he desires. First, when a person needs, it is the lack of X *per se* which causes him harm. Therefore, if what causes a person harm is the frustration of his desire for X rather than the lack of X, then he does not need X. If a person needs X he will be harmed without X whether or not he desires X. If a person is harmed only on the condition that he both lacks and desires X, then we may conclude that it is his desire which causes him the harm. Secondly, if a person needs X, then he will continue to be harmed so long as he lacks it, and he cannot recover without it. But, typically, when the frustration of desire does cause us harm, for instance by making us feel depressed, then we can recover without satisfying the desire.

2 Desires pertain to the motivation of action, usually through interaction with a suitable belief. So, whereas desires will involve an increased disposition to do whatever will bring about what is desired, need is not related directly to action. There may be no tendency to pursue what one needs, and therefore the criterial evidence for need and desire is different. The evidence for a need is the unalterability of a causal link between a lack and harm. Obviously a person's needs will tend to produce action if he knows what he needs. But I may not know what I need, and lack the determination or inclination to act on such knowledge even if I had it.

3 Usually a person knows what he desires, and, because of this, avowals are important evidence in ascertaining what someone desires. Of course, desires can be unconscious, and we are all subject to cravings without knowing what we are craving for. A person is usually aware of what he desires, but, he can be mistaken and ignorant about his needs in many ways. First, one may be mistaken about what one needs: one may know that one needs

water without knowing that one needs H_2O. A person can know that failure to drink will result in death, but not know that it is the failure to drink water that will do this. If needs form extensional contexts, then objects of need can be redescribed *salva veritate*, so long as the descriptions are true in virtue of the obtaining of the same state of affairs. Since 'knowledge that' forms an intensional context, a person can know what he needs under one description and not under another. Secondly, as well as being mistaken about what one needs, one can be ignorant that one needs. For instance, a person may have never lacked what he needs and be ignorant of how this lack would affect him. Also, even if a person does lack what he needs, he may be ignorant of the fact that he is harmed, because harm does not have to be felt in a phenomenological sense. Thirdly, a person might mistake an addiction or a dependence for a fundamental need. In short, beliefs about needs are more complex than the corresponding beliefs about desire, and so when a person says that he needs X, we may not take his utterance as evidence of this, even if he is sincere.

4 Desires are often a function of belief in a way that needs are not. If I believe that X is desirable and available, then I may acquire a desire for it, and when my beliefs about what is desirable change, my desires alter. On the other hand, needs are not a function of belief in this way. My need for X is independent of my beliefs about the desirability of X; it depends on the actual desirability of X.

5 In a sense, desiring and wanting are mental acts. In its least dispositional form, to desire X is to choose that X should come about. Typically, desires which are not easily construed as acts of choice, desires which assail us, involve a phenomenological element: for instance, they are desires which involve feelings of longing or attraction. Needs are never mental acts, but are passive dispositions to suffer certain harms because of certain lacks. There is no act of needing water. Neither do needs involve feelings of need; of course if a person lacks the water he needs then he will feel thirsty, but this is not part of what it means to need water. Typically desiring is something we do, or desires are felt, neither is true of needs. This point is significant with regard to the claim that needs and desires increase in richer societies. Here it is important to distinguish need and desire. As we prosper, we desire more and more, we yearn, feel the pull of desire, think longingly of things, feel attracted, and think 'I must have X' and 'I must buy Y'. This is a

change in the number of desires we have and not in the number of our needs. However, our needs do increase as society grows more complex. For example, to eat one needs money, money has to be earned, but to work it may be necessary to own a car. We can imagine a situation in which a person needs derivatively to own a car in order to live. If our needs increase in this way as society becomes more complex, then this is a change in our derivative, circumstantial needs and not in basic needs. Both basic and derivative needs should be distinguished from desires.

6 Certain inferences that are arguably valid for 'needs' are clearly invalid for 'desires':

If A needs X and if X = Y then A needs Y.

If inferences of this form are valid for 'need', this is because 'need' - statements assert that one state of affairs is causally necessary for the obtaining of another, and because such statements form extensional contexts.[3] It is the one state of affairs which is necessary for the other, and this is true whatever true description we give of that state of affairs. On the other hand, desires are directed to a state of affairs under a particular description, and may not be directed to the same state of affairs under another description. Desires are intentional, and this prevents inference of the above form being valid when we substitute 'desires' for 'needs'.

II

The thesis 'needs override desires' appears to be obviously true when we consider that 'need' claims are recognisably more forceful than 'desire' claims. The term 'need' draws the listener's attention to facts of importance, and the term 'desire' draws attention to the fact that something is desired, however whimsically and fleetingly. 'Need' is more forceful than 'desire' because the concept of a need is tied to the notion of serious harm and the concept of a desire is not.

Some writers are suspicious of this difference in rhetorical and persuasive power between 'need' and 'desire'.[4] They argue that the rhetorical force of 'need' can be used to deny people their freedom to satisfy their desires as they choose, and can be an instrument of oppression. 'Need' is indicted with having authoritarian implications, first because 'need' claims are stronger in force than 'desire' claims, and second because people can be ignorant and mistaken about their needs, but not usually about their desires. These points are correct, of course, but the emphasis and impression is wrong. What writers like Flew and Fitzgerald fail to point out is that we should distinguish proper and improper uses of 'need' and that when 'need' is used properly its rhetorical force is well-grounded.[5] It is only when the term is misused that we should attack its persuasive power as unfounded. For instance, if 'need' is used as equivalent to 'strongly desire', this is a misuse because needs are not strong desires. Furthermore, even when 'need' is used properly, in keeping with the logic of the term, this does not condone authoritarian uses of the term to deny others their freedom. Perhaps people should always be free to act against their own interests and needs, even if it is irrational for them to do so. Thirdly, it should be mentioned that 'need' is not unique in being a possible instrument of oppression. Almost every value term can be so used. These points suggest, not that political thinkers should dispense with the concept of a need because it is inherently confusing, as Fitzgerald seems to say,[6] but that such thinkers, if they do employ the concept of a need, should treat the term cautiously and be alert for ambiguities.

Even if 'need' claims are more forceful than 'desire' claims, this does not mean that needs necessarily override desires. The concept of a need involves the idea of seriousness and the concept of a desire does not. This explains the respective strength of the two types of claim, but it does not rule out the possibility that a desire might be serious and indeed more serious than a need. I shall now examine the thesis that needs override desires, and shall concentrate on the intra- rather than inter-personal case. The thesis 'needs override desires' should be treated with some caution. First, we should beware of treating the thesis with too much importance. It is natural to think that the contrast between 'needs' and 'desires' is all-encompassing: that anything of concern to a person should be categorised either as a need or as a desire, and that things in the first category should have priority over things in the second. But undue emphasis on the 'need'/'desire' contrast can make our conceptual resources appear more impoverished than they really are. For instance, many things that a person loves, cherishes, is committed to and takes an interest in are inadequately regarded as simply desires. Furthermore, needs are indispensable, and as such should be contrasted with the dispensable or that which we can do without, luxuries. Arguably this latter contrast is more basic to the concept of a need than the 'need'/'desire' contrast, and the claim that needs override desires should be explained on the assumption that desire satisfaction for its own sake comes close to being a paradigm instance of a luxury.

There is a second reason for treating the thesis with caution. The thesis that needs override desires appears to be an obvious conceptual truth, and it is tempting to launch into an explanation of this, for instance, by arguing that needs pertain to serious harm and the frustration of a desire does not in itself constitute harm. However, such attempts are likely to be unsuccessful because the thesis itself can be read in different ways. Therefore, the way forward is to distinguish various different claims, which might otherwise be confused, and look for one claim which arguably is a necessary truth.

First, there is the claim that what we need is always more important than what we desire. This claim is demonstrably false. Needs can be rationally overridden and this need overriding action can be the object of a person's desires, and therefore, an object of desire can be more important than an object of need. For example, if, all things considered, a person ought to sacrifice his own health, well-being or life for the sake of others or in the name of some cause, and if he desires to do so, then something which he desires to do is more important than his personal needs. However, the claim that what we need is always more important than what we desire is not a very natural reading of the thesis 'needs override desires', because this latter thesis seems to require that we compare needs and desires as values. If this is so, to refute the thesis 'needs override desires', it is not enough to show that something desired can have rational priority over something needed. It must be shown that, in some sense, needs are always better reasons than desires.

Therefore, many of the putative counter-examples to the thesis 'needs override desires' are not obviously such.[7] For example, a painter might need to give up painting to avoid serious illness, but he does not want to stop his work, and, all things considered, he ought to continue. To show that this is an example of a desire being a better reason than a need, it would have to be argued that (1) the painter did not need to continue his work, and (2) the value of his continuing to work is because he wants to do so. For instance if the example trades on the idea that the painter needs to work, because otherwise his life would become a wreck, or hollow and meaningless, then the example fails to show that desires are better reasons than needs. Even if the painter does not need to continue working for his own sake, it still has to be shown that the value of his work is based on his desire to continue. Clearly the claim that what we need is always more important than what we desire is distinct from the thesis that needs override desires. Since the first is obviously false, anyone who confused the two would reject the second out of hand.

So, we must compare needs and desires as reasons. The thesis we should consider is: 'the value of something needed, where this value is due to the fact that it is needed, is always greater than the value of something desired, when this value is due to the fact that it is desired.' It might be argued that the earlier example of a painter can be a counter-instance to this new, second claim. Let us grant that the painter does not need to continue his work, that he will not be harmed if he does give it up, and that he will be harmed if he does not give it up. Let us also grant that, all things considered, the painter ought to continue his work, despite the sacrifice to his welfare that this will involve. The question remains 'Is the value of his continuing to paint due to the fact that he wants to?' If the answer to this question is affirmative, then the example does constitute a counter-instance to the second reading of the thesis 'needs override desires'. If the answer is negative, the example is not a counter-instance to this second thesis. In one sense, the answer must be negative, because the value of his continuing to paint is not solely and simply because he desires to so do. For as long as a person has the appropriate skills, capacities, and interests, painting is worthwhile whether one wants to do so or not. If this were not the case, then it would be impossible to say that a potential artist ought to take up painting although he does not want to, and it would be impossible to say that a painter who is not all suited to his work ought to give it up, although he does not want to. The value of painting is not simply and solely due to the fact that a person wants to paint, and for this reason the example does not provide a counter-instance to the thesis. This can be argued, even if it is held that desired objects do have some value simply because they are desired, or, in other words, if it is held that X is more valuable for being desired. Of course, if it is held that desire is never a value or reason then the thesis 'needs override desires' is true by default:

needs are better reasons than desires because desires are not reasons.

So far we have rejected the claim that the value of X simply and solely because X is desired can be greater than the value of Y simply and solely because Y is needed. In other words, we have rejected the claim that desires are sufficient to create need-overriding reasons. However, it might be argued that desire can be necessary for need-overriding reasons. This claim should not be confused with the stronger statement that desire is always necessary for need-overriding reasons. For instance, we might wish to separate instances where a person has a moral duty to sacrifice his own life or welfare, whether he wants to or not, from cases where a person has to want to sacrifice his own welfare and where he does not have a desire-independent duty to do so. There is a plausible argument for the weaker claim that desire can be necessary for need-overriding reasons. Let us modify the example of the painter. Suppose that an artist does not need to work, but he has the capacities, skills and interests that befit a good painter. Suppose further that he could equally well be a writer: he would derive as much enjoyment and be equally good and successful as a writer. However, he is committed to painting as an art form and not to writing. One might maintain with plausibility that it would not be irrational for him to continue painting, even when this involves a considerable sacrifice in health and well-being; the same is not true of writing. This is because he is committed to painting as an art form, and not to writing. In other words, commitment can be necessary for the value of his continuing to paint to override the value of his personal needs. In the case of writing, even though all other things are equal, this commitment is lacking, and this is why it would be irrational of him to sacrifice his own needs for the sake of writing. Being committed to an activity and wanting to continue it are not exactly the same. But if we waive this point, and use the term 'desire' rather generously, we can argue that desire can be necessary for a value to override a need.

Clearly, this argument does not require us to abandon the thesis that desires are not sufficient for need-overriding value, and in this sense it remains true that needs are better reasons than desires. But, strangely enough, the claim that desire can be necessary for need-overriding value does not even require the thesis that desire confers some value on its objects. One might maintain that two activities or causes have equal value and worth and that commitment was necessary for that value to have meaning to the subject. In other words, one could maintain that desire never creates value but that desire was sometimes necessary for the subject to latch on to value that was already there – in which case, desire would be like a door to already existing values without creating value.

There is a fourth interpretation of the thesis 'needs override desires', which is that the value of desire satisfaction for its own sake is always less than the value of obtaining what one needs. 'The value of desire satisfaction for its own sake' means simply 'the value of recognising that one has got what one wanted'. This claim is distinct from the claim discussed earlier that desired objects have value because they are desired. The first pertains to the value of recognising that one has got what one desired; the second pertains to the value of things which are desired. If desire satisfaction *per se* is valuable, this is because, all other things being equal, people like having their desires satisfied.[8] We like having our desires satisfied because we perceive the recognition that our will has obtained as valuable. It is as if we said: 'This is what my will has directed and now my will has obtained: this is valuable'. In this sense, desire satisfaction for its own sake is quite different from achievement, where one has struggled and succeeded, because one's desires may be satisfied by accident. Furthermore, the recognition that one's will has obtained may not cause feelings of pleasure and joy. The belief that desire satisfaction for its own sake is valuable is the belief that the recognition that one has got what one wants is valuable, even if that does not cause feelings of joy.

If desire satisfaction for its own sake is not at all valuable, then this interpretation of the thesis 'needs override desires' is true by default. If desire satisfaction is valuable, then I think that it is only a minor or trivial value. For, usually what we desire has value independently of the fact that it is desired, and therefore the obtaining of what we desire has value quite apart from the value of desire satisfaction for its own sake. When we consider this latter value in isolation, it becomes clear how trivial it is. For instance, suppose that what a person wants has no, or almost no, value. If desire satisfaction is valuable, then the subject's recognition that he has got what he wanted is valuable, even when what he wants has no value itself. For this reason I claim that desire satisfaction for its own sake is a trivial minor value and, that the fourth interpretation of the thesis 'needs override desires' is obviously true, and rather unexciting. However, that is what we were after: a dull and obviously true reading of the thesis, the most serious challenge to which is not that desires can be more important than needs, but that desires count for nothing at all.

VIII

IS AND OUGHT

Hare implies that . . . men can choose what they
will take to be fundamental human needs.

W. Hudson[1]

I

Ross Fitzgerald complains that 'need' is an evaluative concept in
empirical disguise.[2] For this reason, he sees the rhetorical force of
'need' as dangerous and ultimately baseless. According to Fitzgerald, the factual component of the concept 'need' can never be
logical ground for its evaluative force, because the factual and
evaluative components of the concept are logically distinct: no
truth-functional combination of factual 'is' statements can ever
entail an evaluative 'ought'. Fitzgerald argues that 'need' is deceptive because it appears to be a bridge between 'is' and 'ought'.

Fitzgerald tows the prescriptivist party line in an uncritical manner, because of his suggestion that the concept of a need is deceptive
and defective.[3] He says: 'The ambiguous notion "need" amalga-
mates and confuses "is" and "ought".'[4] He also says that the
concept of a need involves a conjunction of 'is' and 'ought', and this
is his considered view. But if the concept involves a conjunction of
'is' and 'ought', then it does not confuse them. Even granted his
prescriptivist premises, Fitzgerald's attack on the concept of a need
is unwarranted. According to prescriptivist doctrine, most of our
evaluative concepts involve distinct factual and normative compo-

108

nents, and so 'need' is not especially deceptive for this reason, unless all so-called 'Janus' concepts are deceptive. Perhaps Fitzgerald has in mind the point that Minogue[5] makes that, in a political context, the term 'need' has a strong rhetorical force which can be abused to deprive people of their freedom, and which can become an instrument of oppression. But 'need' is not special in this way either: terms like 'good', 'important', can also be misused in this way.

Rather than attacking the concept of a need, Fitzgerald ought to be attacking those political thinkers who, according to him, misuse the concept. Some writers do assume that 'need' bridges the 'is'–'ought' gap without explaining how or why. Maslow, for instance, says that knowledge of human needs enables us to establish values which have objective validity.[6] The central issue of contention between writers like Fitzgerald, on the one hand, and writers like Maslow, on the other, is whether there is a logical gap between 'is' and 'ought'. However, it does not seem reasonable to claim that the concept of a need by itself can decide this issue. 'Need' does not bridge the 'is'–'ought' gap. If there is such a gap, as prescriptivists maintain, then 'need' is not going to bridge it, because the concept of a need involves both 'is' and 'ought'. On the other hand, if there is no such gap, then 'need' is not required to bridge it. In other words, if value statements are true or false, then it is still not the case that knowledge of human needs by itself is going to establish values of objective validity. Instead, 'need'-claims will be objective because they depend on objective values, rather than providing them.

These points make it clear that the concept of a need by itself cannot settle the 'is'-'ought' question, because that question itself occurs with regard to the concept of a need. Nevertheless, there are reasons for thinking that the 'is'-'ought' question arises in a slightly different way with regard to 'need' than it does with regard to moral concepts. First, writers like Foot and Warnock[7] argue that not anything can count as a morality because a morality must serve human interests and needs. If needs and interests are a factual matter which provide us with reasons for action, then we may approach the question of the nature of moral reasons in the knowledge that interests and needs are factual. If, on the other hand, what counts as a need and an interest involves a free prescriptive element, then, even if it can be shown that morality must serve those interests, this will not remove a prescriptive element from morality. In this sense, the 'is'–'ought' question occurs at a more basic level with regard to concepts like interests and needs than it does with regard to moral concepts. Secondly, the basic issue in the 'is'–'ought' debate is whether certain facts can be reasons. The question of whether my own interests and needs present me with a reason for action seems more basic, and perhaps less complex, than the question of whether my uttering the words 'I promise' in a certain context does. The former question will certainly be more basic than the latter if part of the value of the promise-keeping institution is the way it serves human interests. Of course, we cannot hope to understand the reason we have not to damage other people's interests, unless we have some grasp of the nature of the reason each person has to avoid damaging his own interests. This shows that the 'is'–'ought' debate occurs at a more basic level with regard to prudential concepts than it does with regard to moral concepts. It does not show, however, that 'need' is any more special than any other prudential concept. What makes 'need' special is that paradigmatically needs are inescapable. This means that, whilst the argument form 'A loves X, but X is not good, because A ought not to love X' is valid for, say, 'loves' and 'desires', the parallel argument for 'need' is not valid. At least for the paradigm instances of 'need', it is inappropriate to ask whether A ought to need X, for this presupposes that A has some choice in this matter.

Granted that 'need' is not going to settle the 'is'–'ought' debate, we still have to defend the assumption made in this book that the concept of a need should not be analysed prescriptively.[8] Certain arguments have already been given to support this assumption. First, as it is usually stated, prescriptivism implies that we can choose what our fundamental needs are. For example, Dearden says:

> 'Needs'-statements are rebutted, not by adducing certain facts, but by rejecting the norms being presupposed. . . . I may refuse to attach importance to health. . .[9]

What is revealing about this quotation is the talk of 'attaching importance'. Of course, we may refuse to believe that something is important, and we may refuse to value it, though usually we have reasons for so doing. But none of this shows that through an act of refusal, health becomes unimportant, nor that through some act of acceptance health becomes important. However, Dearden does mean that we can just reject the norms being presupposed by a 'need' claim, and that such norms 'can neither be discovered nor refuted empirically'. Since the norms involved in 'need'-claims pertain to individual harm and well-being, this means that we can choose the nature of harm. And, since there is no factual evidence relevant to such choice, constraining how we ought to choose, the nature of harm is indefinitely plastic. In other words, it is a real possibility that harm to an individual could consist in his being deprived of illness, friendlessness, boredom, etc. – all depending on which norms he accepts and rejects, or on how he chooses. In opposition to this, I have argued that needs are inescapable,[10] and that this requires the rejection of the type of view put forward by Dearden. In support of this argument, I have advanced an alternative view of harm, which accommodates the claim that needs arc inescapable, and which explains the value of avoiding harm in terms of the empirical content of the concept 'harm'.

Secondly, Hare contends that to be harmed is to be deprived of what one desires,[11] and that, since 'desire' is a prescriptive notion, the concept of harm is also prescriptive. Since we have already rejected a desire-based view of harm in favour of an interest-based account, we can reject Hare's view of harm. However, this is not in itself an argument against a prescriptive theory of harm, unless reasons can be found for thinking that the notion of an interest is not amenable to an imperative analysis. There is some plausibility in maintaining that to desire X is to prescribe X. This is because to prescribe X is like coming to a decision or making a choice, and in this respect has something in common with desiring. In contrast, having an interest is not at all like making a choice, and for this reason it is implausible to maintain that having an interest in X is to prescribe X. In short, it is precisely the differences between desires and interests and the similarities between desiring and prescribing, which make it implausible to regard the having of an interest as the assent to a self-addressed imperative. However, these two arguments are unlikely to carry much weight on their own, and for this reason I would like to supplement them with a more general argument, which attacks the notion of prescriptive force. Before that, however, I would like to make a final point.

We must be careful to characterise the issue between a prescriptive and a descriptive analysis of 'need' in the right way. In particular, we must not apply the prescriptive analysis prematurely, for otherwise the analysis will be less informative than it could be. For instance, take the claim that to say 'I need X' is to prescribe X. Although 'need' can be used to recommend its logical object, even if one thinks of this recommendation prescriptively, this is not an adequate analysis of the central use of 'need'. For 'need' is linked to the notion of an inescapable necessary condition. A more informative, less premature application of the prescriptivist analysis would be to say that 'I need X' is used to state that X is indispensably necessary for the achievement of certain ends and to prescribe the fulfilment of those ends. Although this analysis is more informative than the first, even it is premature, because it could be more informative about the nature of the ends. Suppose we say that needs are inescapably necessary to avoid serious harm, and characterise the normative element of need as the prescription that one should not be harmed. Even then, we have not elucidated properly the reason we have to avoid harm. More can be said about harm, i.e. that it consists of the deprivation of desirable activities and experiences. It is at this point that the prescriptive analysis should either be applied or denied.

II

It is common-sense to believe that certain facts by themselves provide us with reasons for action: for instance, the fact that X will cause a man pain provides him with a reason for avoiding X, or the fact that a person desires X provides him with a reason for seeking X. Granted that facts can be reasons, it is then natural to analyse some 'ought' statements in terms of reasons: to say that a person ought to do A is to say that he has a reason to do A, which is to make an assertion, to say something true or false in the circumstances.

Prescriptivists will want to deny this. First, they will want to deny that any fact can be a reason, for this would contradict the principle that one cannot derive an 'ought' from an 'is'. They will consequently deny that statements about what one has reason to do are assertions rather than prescriptions. Which of the two accounts are we to accept? Harman argues that the descriptive analysis of reason statements is preferable to the prescriptive analysis, because it can account better for the different strength of reason statements.[12] He claims that the differences between 'ought', 'must' and 'can' are more easily accounted for with a descriptive analysis of reason

112

statements. But Harman does not push this argument far enough. The point can be developed into a two-stage argument; the first stage concerns conclusive reasons, the second what are often called 'prima facie' reasons (although this is a misnomer). The culminative effect of this argument is to show that reasons for action cannot be analysed prescriptively.

The argument requires that we characterise prescriptive force and distinguish it from descriptive force. That there is a difference in kind between prescriptive and descriptive force depends on the fact that prescriptions have much in common with simple impera- tives. Whereas assenting to a description is to believe, assenting to a prescription is analogous to obeying a command, and to obey a command is to act as the command directs. This is the root of the claimed difference between prescriptive and descriptive force. As Hare says:

> An indicative sentence is used for telling someone that something is the case; an imperative is not – it is used for telling someone to make something the case.[13]

Hare does not claim that prescriptions are imperatives, but rather that they entail imperatives. To assent to a prescription is to assent to an imperative, and if a person assents to the imperative 'let me do A', then he must do A if he is able to. If he does not do A and he was able to, then either his assent to the imperative was insincere, or he did not understand what he was doing when he gave his assent. Given that none of these conditions hold, it is contradictory to suppose that a person could assent sincerely to an imperative and not act as the imperative directs.[14]

Given this, if we analyse 'P has a reason to do A' as entailing his assent to the imperative 'let me do A', then it seems that the reason statement must be a conclusive reason statement. This is because it is essential to the notion of a (*prima facie*) reason that a person P can recognise that he has such a reason to do A and yet fail to do A, without being inconsistent, insincere, weak or stupid. He can recognise that he has a reason to do A and not do A, although he is able to, and without insincerity, etc., because he recognises that he has a better reason to do B. Thus, as it stands, there is a disparity between assent to a prescription and recognising that one has a reason for action. The disparity is that, whereas the first requires action, the second may not. Therefore, it seems that the Harean analysis of reason statements could be only plausible for the case of conclusive reasons for action, and cannot be suitable as it stands for the notion of a reason. This is because assent to an imperative is too closely tied to action to capture the weaker notion of a reason.

The weaker notion is more important in giving general character-isations of concepts like 'need', than that of a conclusive reason. In general, we can say that our needs present us with a reason for action, and it is this notion which is required to analyse the normative nature of the concept of a need. To say that needs are conclusive reasons for action is to say something too strong, because needs can be overridden. The statement 'I have a reason to satisfy my needs' may be an analytic or conceptual truth, but it is not universally true that a person has a conclusive reason to satisfy his needs. This is enough to show that the concept of a need cannot be analysed simply in the usual imperatival way.

Essentially the same point can be made about the whole range of desirability concepts. Notions like honesty, courage, and generosity are all inadequately represented by the usual prescriptive analysis, because, as it stands, that analysis is only suitable to capture the nature of a conclusive reason for action. We cannot analyse the normative nature of these concepts in terms of conclusive reasons for action. The view that facts can never be reasons for action because an 'ought' cannot be derived from an 'is' derives much support from the failure to separate clearly reasons and conclusive reasons. The relationship between a reason statement and an 'is' could be quite different from the relationship between a conclusive 'ought' and an 'is' statement. If these relationships are different, then the putative fact/value gap could be quite different from the putative 'is'/'ought' gap, although few philosophers distinguish between them. For instance, if needs provide us with reasons for action, then the statement that A needs X will entail the statement that he has a reason to seek X. Similarly for desire. In each case, a statement of fact will entail a value judgment. One could hold that this was the case, and yet still hold no finite set of factual statements pertaining to people's desires and needs will ever entail a conclusive 'ought'. Suppose that one accepts the definition of a conclusive reason or 'ought' as follows: person P ought to do A in situation S if and only if P has a reason to do A, and there is no alternative action B in situation S such that P has a better reason to do B than he has to do A, all things considered. If one accepts this definition of 'ought', then it is clear that there is a sort of gap between statements of the form 'P desires X' and 'P needs X', and conclusive oughts. However, this gap is not of the kind described by prescriptivists, and the existence of this gap is consistent with some facts being reasons for action or values. If the above definition is correct, then the gap between finite statements of fact and conclusive 'oughts' exists because conclusive 'oughts' depend on an unbounded negative existential.

The first stage of the argument showed that, as it stands, prescriptivist theory can give a suitable analysis of conclusive reason statements only: i.e. 'Let me do A' is only a reasonable analysis of 'I have a conclusive reason to do A'. Given this point, the prescriptivist must find a way to adapt his analysis to include non-conclusive reason statements. The second part of my analysis is to show that this cannot be done.

How are we to modify the imperatival analysis so that it can cater for non-conclusive reasons? One suggestion is that we should elucidate non-conclusive reasons in terms of conditional imperatives of the form

Let me do A unless C_1 or C_2 . . . or C_n

The idea behind this suggestion is that if a person P assents to this conditional imperative, then, when the whole C series is false, he has a conclusive reason to do A, and, when any one or more of the C series is true, he has a non-conclusive reason to do A. When one of the C series is true, P can assent to the imperative and fail to do A without inconsistency, insincerity, etc., and, in this sense, he has a reason to do A which is non-conclusive. According to this suggestion, the conditional imperative is supposed to capture or represent the notion of a non-conclusive reason, because it frames a rule which specifies exactly when P does and does not have a conclusive reason to do A.

However, anyone who adopts this suggestion faces a serious problem. The conditional prescription is supposed to specify exactly when P can fail to do A without insincerity, etc., whilst at the same time assenting to the imperative. This means that the C series specified in the 'unless' clause must be complete. The 'unless' clause must specify completely all the possible states of affairs, such that if any one of them were true, then P would have a conclusive reason to do other than A. Suppose the C series specified in the 'unless' clause

115

were incomplete, then circumstances could arise in which P has a conclusive reason to do other than A, and yet in those circumstances P is committed to the prescription 'Let me do A'. So, the specififed C series must be complete, but the problem is that it seems impossible to meet this requirement. Complex conditional principles of the above kind are open-ended.

Let us make this point more concrete. Suppose P assents to the prescription 'Let me do what ensures my continued survivial'. Thus, he is commited logically to doing just that, and if he finds himself in a situation where he has a better reason to do something else and sacrifice his own life, then he must alter the imperative to which he assents. He must assent to a principle of the form:

Let me do A unless. . . .

However, a person can lay down his life for indefinitely many reasons, and thus it seems a hopeless task to try to complete the 'unless' clause in the required way. There are an indefinite number of states of affairs which could require a person to sacrifice his own life. This can be seen from the following dilemma. In attempting to make a list of all such possible states of affairs, we must use either more or less specific descriptions. The more specific the description used, the more difficult it becomes to complete such a list, because the more and more variety will have to be incorporated in it. To give one general reading for C: 'action A will lead to the horrific death of several persons close to my heart'. When one considers the multifarious specific descriptions this could encompass, it becomes obvious that the more specific our descriptions are, the more difficult it becomes to complete the list. This might lead us to suppose that we can complete the list in the required way of using more general descriptions. However, this supposition turns out to be false too, for with general terms there will always be the possibility that cases arise where the applicability of the words is in question. This is because with a general word 'no firm convention or general agreement dictates its use'.[15] Because no firm rules can exist which legislate in advance the applicability of the general term to every possible case, one cannot secure an exhaustive list. So we have a dilemma: if we turn to specific descriptions, we encounter the impossibility of foreseeing and accounting for every possible combination of circumstances in framing the rule. If, on the other hand, we resort to general descriptions, we run against the fact that

116

general terms do not carry rules whose applicability is established by the rule itself.

A further point needs to be made. For the prescriptivist, the terms which we use to complete the list must be purely factual or neutral. For if the terms have an evaluative component, then this must be separable from the factual and must itself be amenable to prescriptive analysis. Since the evaluative component of most normative concepts is not adequately characterised in terms of conclusive reasons for action and hence also simple prescriptions, the same problems will then occur with regard to that evaluative element.

The reason why the conditional imperative cannot be used to analyse the notion of a reason is that the conditional prescription tries to frame a rigid rule which specifies exactly when a person has conclusive reason to do other than A. I have argued that such a rule is in principle unframable, and thus cannot be used to analyse the notion of a (*prima facie*) reason. Part of the problem is that the conditional rule is designed to transcend all contexts. Independently of context, we cannot hope to specify when a person does and does not have a conclusive reason for action of a certain type. This is because a (*prima facie*) reason can operate in an indefinite number of contexts, including those which have never been thought of. This is why, when we try to characterise in general terms the reason we have to fulfil our needs, it is easy to say something too strong, if we go beyond the claim that our needs present us with a reason for action.

The first stage of the argument showed that imperatival prescriptions provide a suitable analysis of conclusive reasons only: i.e. 'Let me do A' can only be a plausible analysis of 'I have a conclusive reason to do A'. The notion of a conclusive reason is too strong to capture in general terms the evaluative component of most normative concepts. The second stage of the argument showed that one cannot analyse 'I have a reason to do A' in terms of the conditional imperative 'Let me do A unless . . .' For the conclusion to follow that prescriptivists cannot adequately elucidate the weaker notion of a reason, we must show that there is no other avenue of suitable analysis. There are good grounds for thinking that there is no such avenue. Given our earlier points, the prescriptivist is committed to take the notion of a conclusive reason as in some way prior to the notion of a reason. From the concept of a conclusive reason elucidated imperatively, he must somehow derive the weaker notion of a reason. This cannot be done, because the notion of a reason is in a sense more basic than that of a conclusive reason: in a way, a conclusive reason is a type of reason, but a reason is not a type of conclusive reason. This must be explained. A conclusive reason should be defined as follows: a person P has a conclusive reason to do A in situation S if and only if P has a reason to do A in S, and there is no alternative action B, such that P has a better reason to do B than he does A, all things considered. This definition makes it clear in what sense a conclusive reason is a type of reason. The notion of a reason encompasses both conclusive and overridden reasons, in the sense that, in a particular situation, if something is a reason then it must be either a conclusive or an overridden reason. But, what is an overridden reason in one situation may be a conclusive reason in another. Thus we cannot assign a reason into the conclusive or overridden types except in a particular context.

In his early works, Hare does not discuss the notion of a *prima facie* principle, and there is little to indicate how he would respond to the above arguments.[16] In his most recent work, he does discuss the concept of a *prima facie* principle and its relation to a prescriptivism, although much of this work is not directly relevant to the meta-ethical problems raised here, because it is addressed to the need for a distinction between intuitive and critical levels of moral thinking and not meta-ethics.

According to Hare, we come to a situation or moral conflict with intuitively held *prima facie* principles, which are formally speaking universal prescriptions. In a situation where two such principles conflict, we cannot obey them both, and 'the problem is to determine which of these principles should be applied to yield a prescription for this specific situation.'[17] In the situation, one of the principles has to be overridden by the other, without them being altered or qualified. According to Hare, the principle which is overridden is simply not applied in this case. He says:

> This overridability does not mean that they are not prescriptive; if applied, they would require a certain action, but we just do not apply them in a certain case.[18]

But can one hold a principle and not apply it? It seems not if to hold a principle is to assent to an imperative, because to assent to an imperative is to act as it directs. To hold the principle 'Never kill' is to apply it, and one cannot hold that principle and yet not apply it in a particular circumstance. For this reason, Hare's *prima facie* prescriptive principles must be of the form 'Sometimes do not kill', for one can accept such a principle and not apply it in a particular instance.

The thesis under consideration now is that *prima facie* principles can be represented by prescriptions of the form 'Sometimes do A'. This seems to be what Hare has in mind when he says:

> The *prima facie* principles are general in two connected senses: they are simple and unspecific, and they admit of exceptions, in the sense that it is possible to go on holding them while allowing that in particular cases one may break them. . . . In other words, they are overridable.[19]

However, contrary to what Hare suggests, to say that one has made an exception to a principle is not the same as saying that it is overridden, because one can make a random, *ad hoc*, and reasonless exception to a principle, that is, break it without adequate reason. The person who assents to the principle 'Sometimes do not kill' or 'In some circumstances do not kill' can in all consistency perform random, *ad hoc* killings without adequate reason. The person who believes that there is a reason against killing is, on his own admission, acting irrationally if he kills without believing that he has a reason for so doing, and without believing that this reason is better than the reason against killing. Thus, in opposition to Hare, I contend that *prima facie* principles are of the form 'There is a reason to do A' or 'There is a reason against doing A', and, therefore, that such principles should be analysed in terms of the concept of a reason for action. Hare rejects this claim, because he tries to analyse the notion of an overridden *prima facie* principle in terms of one's making an exception to that principle. Clearly, one can accept a principle of the form 'There is a reason to do A' and treat it as overridden in a particular context, without making an exception to that principle. Furthermore, I contend that the notion of a reason cannot be analysed imperatively, and in particular that the principle 'There is a reason to do A' cannot be analysed as the prescription 'Sometimes do A', nor as one's making exceptions to the prescription 'Do A'.

Since Hare rejects the claim that *prima facie* principles require the notion of a reason, perhaps Hare would reject the notion of a reason altogether, and adopt what we can call the 'Ross view of reasons'.[20] According to this view, a *prima facie* principle is just that – a candidate principle, or what appears at first sight to be a principle, and a *prima facie* reason should be regarded in the same way. In this sense of the phrase, '*prima facie*' should be contrasted with 'real' and not conclusive. In this sense, a *prima facie* reason need not be a reason at all: 'I have a *prima facie* reason to do A' does not entail 'I have a reason to do A', because it is consistent with 'It only appears that I have a reason to do A'. Following Searle,[21] I would like to make three points about this view.

First, according to 'the Ross view', there is no conflict of reasons. Normally we should describe a conflict of reasons as follows. There is a reason for person P to do both A and B but he cannot do both. Hence, there is a conflict of reasons and P must resolve this conflict by trying to discover which of the two reasons is stronger or better. According to the Ross view, this situation does not involve any conflict of reasons because *prima facie* it appears that there is a reason for P to do both A and B, but in fact, there can only be reason for him to perform one of these actions, say A. If there is a reason for P to do A, then there is no reason at all for him to do B, and so there is no conflict of reasons. Contrary to what Searle says,[22] this does not seem to be a conclusive argument against the Ross view, because, although there is no conflict of reasons, P does face the problem of trying to establish which of the two apparent reasons is real, and it might be argued that this is an adequate characterisation of what we regard as a conflict of reasons.

Secondly, Hare talks of one *prima facie* reason overriding another, and this is inconsistent with his adopting the Ross view. The Ross view allows no room for the notion of a reason which can be overridden, and thus cannot accommodate the idea that one reason is better or stronger than another. If we reject the Ross view, we can say that the reason person P has to do A in S is stronger than the reason he has to do B in S, even when, all things considered, P ought to do C. According to the Ross view, if P has a reason to do C, he has no reason at all to do either A or B, and therefore he cannot have a better reason to do A than B. On the Ross view, we cannot even say that he has a better reason to do C than A, because it only appears that P has a reason to do A. In other words, the view is inconsistent with the claim that one reason can override another, or can be stronger or more important than another. This means that the view cannot capture the variety and complexity of things that we wish to say about a conflict of reasons. For instance, it becomes impossible to say that needs are better reasons than desires.

Thirdly, according to the Ross view, actual reasons should be contrasted with what appear to be reasons, or apparent reasons. According to Hare, the statement 'I have a non *prima facie* reason to do A in situation S' should be analysed prescriptively. Thus P has a reason to do A in S if and only if he assents to the imperative 'Let me do A in S'. Because this assent requires action, the notion of an actual reason comes close to the concept of a conclusive reason. If Hare's adoption of the Ross view implies that all reasons are akin to conclusive reasons, then we are still faced with the problem set at the beginning of the section: 'How are we to give a general characterisation of the recommendatory nature of most normative concepts in prescriptivist terms?' We cannot say that promises create obligations nor that needs provide us with reasons for action, because the Ross view dispenses with the concept of an overridable reason. Thus, we are back to the old problem of how to say that a person has an overridable reason in prescriptivist terms without saying too much or too little. Hare's adoption of the Ross view merely accentuates this problem, because it involves the rejection of the notion of an overridable reason and replaces it with the concept of an apparent reason. It is too weak to say that promises create *prima facie* obligations, for this means only that they appear to create obligations. Thus, 'the Ross view' 'denies such obvious conceptual truths as that promises create obligations'.[23] But such conceptual truths are needed to characterise the normative nature of concepts like promising, and need.

To conclude, prescriptivism cannot analyse adequately the notion of a reason for action. We cannot analyse the statement 'there is a reason against killing' in terms of the imperative 'Do not kill', nor in terms of the imperative 'Sometimes do not kill', nor in terms of imperative of the form 'Do not kill unless C_1 or C_2 etc.'. If the notion of a reason cannot be analysed imperatively, then prescriptivists must accept the Ross view of reasons, which in effect rejects the notion of an overridable reason. However, this view is not acceptable, because we require the notion of an overridable reason to state conceptual truths like 'promises create obligations' and 'needs provide reasons', and also because we require the notion of one reason being stronger or better than another. In short, we require the notion of an overridable reason for action, and therefore we should reject prescriptivism, and prescriptive analyses of the concept of a fundamental need.

IX

MAKING A VIRTUE OF NECESSITY

Teach thy necessity to reason thus;
there is no virtue like necessity.

Shakespeare

We began this study by noting that needs have a special role in the justification or evaluation of goals and ideals, and by asking why this is so. Tentatively, I claimed that this is because what we need is an objective matter of fact, and because objects of need have an unimpeachable value and are a matter of priority. We should conclude the study of explaining what these claims amount to and by outlining in more detail the role of needs in evaluation.

The main feature of the concept of a need is that it makes a virtue of necessity by cutting down options and thereby simplifying choice. The empirical aspect of the concept is shaped by three general applications of the notion of necessity.

1 The object of a need is necessary in the obvious sense that it is a necessary condition.

2 The need itself is necessary in the extended sense that the subject of the need has it by virtue of his nature: A's need is essential to A. We may read into this three implications, namely that A's need is basic or non- derivative, that it is non-circumstantial, and, finally, that it is inescapable. The third of these implications has the most obvious significance. However, the first two are also important because they determine what type of necessary condition we refer to when

we use the word 'need' in its fundamental sense.[1]

3 The antecedent of a need[2] is necessary in the sense that it is essential to A. 'Need' contains the idea that A needs X to be A or to function as A, and it implies that the 'purpose' for which X is needed by A is defined by A's essential nature. The rich sense of 'need' determines that the antecedent of a 'need'-statement must be A's life or the quality of his life, or more specifically, the avoidance of an especially serious type of harm. By way of the idea of necessity, 'need' in the rich sense of the term also determines that what counts as harm to A must be defined with reference to A's essential and hence inescapable nature.[3]

Needs are also practically necessary in the sense that what we need is indispensable or unforgoable; what we need is something we must have. This is because if A needs X then he is inescapably locked into the position where he must suffer serious harm without it. In using the term 'need', we exploit the notion of natural necessity so as to force our hand practically. Objects of need are practically necessary because they are naturally necessary. The fact that needs are a matter of priority and that true need claims are unimpeachable is a consequence of what needs are, and it is because of this that needs are objective.

1 WHY ARE NEEDS OBJECTIVE?

If a philosopher seeks to define an objective notion of need, then he will be trying to show that it is a determinable matter of fact what needs a person has and that these needs provide their subject and hence others with a reason for action. In short, he will argue that 'need' is at the same time an empirical and an evaluative concept. In support of this position, we have tried to reveal what the empirical content of the concept 'need' is and how this content has value implications. In addition, we have tried to undermine the opposite view at source, concentrating on prescriptivism as the most advanced and persuasive theory of its kind.

Prescriptivism is based largely on two contentions: one, that a version of the open-question argument works, and, second, that all evaluations are prescriptions. At the heart of the open-question argument is the claim that there is a logical gap between 'is' and 'ought' statements. This claim appears plausible for conclusive 'oughts' but not for non-conclusive 'oughts'. Furthermore, the prescriptivist analysis of evaluation is *prima facie* plausible only for conclusive 'ought' statements. Weaker evaluations, like 'A has a reason to do X' and 'A has a strong reason to do X' cannot be analysed prescriptively. Yet it is these weaker evaluations we require to elucidate the concept of a need, because the statement 'A needs X' does not entail 'A has a conclusive reason to seek X'. On these grounds, we can reject the prescriptivist analysis of 'need' and assert with confidence that the empirical statement 'A needs X' does entail 'A has a reason to seek X'.

Thinkers who attempt to give an objective definition of 'need' do so for a reason. Often the reason is that needs are thought to have an important role in establishing the objectivity of other values. The idea is that because needs are a bridge between 'is' and 'ought', disputes concerning other values can be settled empirically with reference to our needs.

However, the suggestion that needs bridge an 'is'/'ought' gap is misleading. The argument against prescriptivism has a general application to evaluative concepts. Consequently, the concept of a need is far from unique in allowing us to infer a reason from a matter of fact, and in this sense, there is no gap to be bridged.

Despite this, there may be an important grain of truth in the claim of those who seek an objective definition of 'need'. If the concept of a need has a clear and determinate empirical content in comparison with other evaluative concepts, like those of beauty, freedom, equality and democracy, then agreement can be more easily reached about what needs people have and disputes concerning needs can be more readily settled empirically. If this is the case, then justifications which cite needs have the attraction that they appeal more clearly to facts.

2 WHY ARE NEEDS UNIMPEACHABLE?

The concept of a need provides a solid basis for evaluation because 'need' claims are invulnerable to certain types of criticism. This does not mean that needs cannot be overridden: a need does not necessarily provide a conclusive reason for action. What it does mean is that our needs present us with strong reasons for action which are not rebutted by other considerations.

First, we cannot truly say that a person ought to have different needs. This is because fundamental needs are inescapable. Consequently, when we justify an ideal or an aim by claiming that it answers certain fundamental needs, we cannot challenge this claim by arguing that the persons concerned ought to have different needs or ought to alter their needs. On the other hand, this challenge is available in the case of desires. It is pertinent to ask whether a person ought to have different desires. If he ought to, then the desires in question cannot be used as a clear and firm basis of evaluating other goals and ideals.

True 'need' claims are immune from another type of challenge. Needs do not depend on any choice or decision that the subject makes. We do not adopt needs in the way we adopt goals or aims. Nor do we adopt the interests which define our needs. Because of this, there can be no question of our adopting the wrong needs nor of our making a bad choice or decision concerning our needs.

Thirdly, the goals we adopt usually depend on our beliefs. For example, suppose a person who has an aim to achieve a certain sales figure has this goal because he believes that he will feel self-respect when he attains his target, and because he believes that he can achieve it without making too many sacrifices. However, if both beliefs happen to be false, he should revise his aim, and that goal cannot be used to justify further aims. On the other hand, needs do not depend on such beliefs. A needs X independently of his beliefs about the desirability and ease of obtaining X. Thus, if we justify an aim by arguing that it answers certain needs, our justification will not be open to the challenge that the needs in question depend on false beliefs.

Much the same point can be made about the interests which define our needs. We do not form such interests from our beliefs about what is a primary good, nor from our beliefs about what constitutes the good life or flourishing. What counts as harm to A does not depend on what A believes counts as harm.

3 WHY ARE NEEDS A MATTER OF PRIORITY?

There are two ways of explaining why needs are a matter of priority:

first, with reference to the content of the concept and, secondly, in comparison with other evaluative notions. The first of these is primary.

Needs are important because the harm suffered by a person when he lacks what he needs is especially serious. In the extreme, a person literally cannot do without what he needs; without it he is deprived of being an agent and a subject of experience at all. In the less extreme case, whilst the subject is not deprived of all primary goods, the deprivation is not confined to a localised or narrow aspect of his life, but rather infects all of it. Such harm must continue so long as the subject lacks what he needs; it is otherwise inescapable. The harm involves the absence of basic types of primary goods rather than the absence of particular goods which can be forgone because they are replaceable. There are no substitutes for the basic categories of primary goods which we are deprived of when we lack what we need. In part this is what we mean when we say that what counts as harm to A depends on A's essential nature.

We also mean that the suffering of such harm is not merely a question of a person's not getting what he specifically wants or desires, but is more a question of his not getting what lies at the root of a whole range of wants. Harm consists in our life-style not meeting the interests which motivate our desires rather than in our desires not being met.

Needs are also important because they are inescapable necessary conditions. Practical inferences which employ such necessary conditions have a unique feature: they preserve the strength of reasons. With inferences of this form the strength of reasons is transmitted from premise to conclusion without being lessened or weakened. For instance, if A has a strong reason to avoid a specific harm and if he inescapably needs X to avoid that harm, then A must have a strong reason to obtain X. In fact, if A absolutely must be harmed without X, then he cannot have a lesser reason to get X than he has to avoid the harm. The first reason must be at least as strong as the second.[5]

This point can be generalised. If what A needs is necessary for him to avoid living an impoverished life, then his needs cannot be less important than the quality of his life. We must treat the two as equal in value, and to this extent we can use them interchangeably. This appears to be a unique feature of the concept 'to need'. It is not true of other prudential concepts, for instance of 'to benefit', 'to advantage', 'to be good for' and 'to be valuable'. Something can be all of these things without being as important as the subject's well-being itself. On the other hand, A's needs must be as important as the quality of the subject's life. The two are equal in value.

Evaluation always has a point or purpose, and this purpose defines the criteria we should use in making the evaluation. For example, Warnock argues that the point of moral evaluation is to ameliorate the human condition by combating the detrimental effects of our limited sympathy and concern for each other.[6] Warnock uses this claim to argue that morality has a necessary content as well as a form and that elucidation of moral concepts requires reference to that content. To explain moral concepts and criteria we must understand the point of moral evaluation.

If the point of an evaluation, whether it be moral, political or prudential, is to improve the quality of people's lives in some respect, then the concept of a need will be tailor-made as a basis for that type of evaluation. Furthermore if what we need cannot be less important than the quality of our lives and if the point of an evaluation is to improve that quality, then objects of need cannot be less important than instances of the concepts we employ in making the evaluation. For example, if the general point behind judging things as fair is that by making such judgments we improve the quality of people's lives, we cannot truly say that fairness is more important than the quality of people's lives.[7] And if we cannot say this, fairness cannot be more important than people's needs. In other words, needs are a matter of priority in comparison with other evaluative concepts because the point of evaluation is to improve the quality of people's lives or to enhance their welfare, and needs cannot be less important than human welfare.

NOTES

CHAPTER I   CLASSIFICATION AND CLARIFICATION

1 See Kenny, 1975, p. 48. In 1982 R. Lindley testified to the continuing truth of Kenny's words: 'the absence of an adequate theory of needs is to say the least conspicuous.' Lindley wrote this in his review of a book by Kate Soper (*On Human Needs*, Harvester, 1981), for the *Times Higher Educational Supplement*, March 1982. Lindley explains that Soper's work does not fill this gap: 'Soper does not try to present such a theory.' Unfortunately, like all the books on 'need', Soper's work does not give an elucidation of the concept, but concentrates on political thought and exegesis; see also Fitzgerald, 1977, and Springborg, 1981.

2 Peters, 1960, p. 17; White, 1975, p. 107; Wollheim, 1975, p. 174; White, 1975, p. 107; Springborg, 1981, p. 252; Peters, 1960, p. 18.

3 White, 1975, p. 106.

4 See, for instance, Flew, 1977, pp. 214–28; Barry, 1965, chapter III; White, 1975.

5 Fowler in *Modern English Usage* says that the phrase 'needs must' is used ironically to express contempt for an action. Fowler cites: 'All the plans were made with great care and he needs must interfere'. The other quote is from II Samuel 14:14.

6 The verb and auxiliary forms of 'need' can be treated together because the verb form 'I need X' can be converted into the auxiliary form 'I need to have X'.

7 See p. 7 and p. 11.

8 Sentences like 'legislation was not only necessary but it was now possible' would be logically odd if 'necessary' did not have these two senses.

9 As do Feinberg in *Social Philosophy*, 1973, p. 111; Anscombe, 'Modern Moral Philosophy', 1958, p. 7 and David Richards, *A Theory of Reasons*

129

for Action, 1970, pp. 37–8. For example, Feinberg says: '. . . to say that S needs X is to say simply that if he doesn't have X he will be harmed.' This ignores the fact that 'need' is a modal notion even when it is normative.

10 'A φs' is the antecedent of the conditional 'If A φs then A has X' which is necessarily true if A needs X to φ.

11 White fails to appreciate the differences between the noun and verb uses of 'need'; he says: ' "If a gas is to explode, it must be touched by a spark" signifies a need', 1975, p. 103. See also p. 104 and the criticisms of White's views by McClosky, 1976, p. 3.

12 See pp. 18–19 on the differences between derivative and non-derivative fundamental needs. I am grateful to David Wiggins for this example.

13 See, for instance, Kai Nielson, 'Morality and Needs', 1969, p. 191 and McCloskey, 1976, p. 3.

14 Or, to reword the famous saying, necessity is other than intention.

15 For an elaboration of this point see Chapter III, pp. 59–61.

16 Among those who claim that 'need' does entail 'lack' are: Wollheim, 1975, p. 174; Sparshott, 1958, p. 133; Komisar, 1961, p. 27; Peters and Hirst, 1970, p. 33. White, 1975, argues that 'need' never entails 'lack'.

17 In *King Lear*, Shakespeare talks of the 'sharp pinch of need' (Act II, Scene 4). To feel a need is to feel the effects of lacking what one needs. The Voltaire quotation is from *Candide*.

18 This use has crept into the Dictionary; 'Need – a state of psychological or physiological want that consciously or unconsciously motivates behaviour towards its satisfaction' (Supplement to the *Oxford English Dictionary*, p. 1153, volume 2, Clarendon, 1976).

19 For instance, K. Koffka: 'Needs are states of tension which persist until they are relieved' (*Principles of Gestalt Psychology*, 1962, p. 329 viii). Freud: 'need . . . a stimulus of instinctoid origin' (1915, p. 62). See also Maslow, 1954, *Motivation and Personality*, especially chapters 4 and 6; Murray, 1938, *Explorations in Personality*, pp. 54–129; Fromm, 1967, *Man for Himself*, p. 46.

20 For criticisms of the theory see: Peters, 1960, pp. 17–26; White, 1975, pp. 116–18; Wright and Taylor, *Introducing Psychology* (Penguin, 1972), pp. 206–9; 'Need in Psychology', in Gould and Kolb (eds), *Dictionary of Social Sciences*, 1964, p. 462.

21 See Springborg, 1981, p. 252.

22 For example see: Bay, 1958, p. 12 & p. 327; 1968, pp. 241–61; 1977, chapter 1; Aronoff, *Psychological Needs and Cultural Systems*, 1967, chapter 1.

23 This view is held by White, 1975; Barry, 1965, pp. 48–9; Flew, 1977, pp. 213–28; Dearden, 1972, p. 50, and is opposed by Miller, *Social Justice*, p. 130.

24 See Flew, *The Politics of Procrustes*, 1981, p. 120: 'If I say that I need something it is never inept to ask what for . . .'

25 As is claimed by P. Taylor, 1959, pp. 107–10.

26 See Hare, 'Wrongness and Harm', 1972, pp. 97–8, and 'Wanting: Some Pitfalls', 1971, p. 51.

27 As R. Fitzgerald claims in Fitzgerald, 1977, p. ix.

CHAPTER II   HUMAN NATURE

1 These quotations are from Seneca, *Epistulae ad Lucilium*, *Epistle* XXXI, 3, and *De Ira*, Book II 1, 20.
2 The opening line of Epictetus's *Encheiridon* is: 'Some things are under our control, while others are not under our control.'
3 'Nature's demands are slight; the demands of opinion are boundless,' says Seneca in *Epistle*, XVI, 7–8.
4 Compare the quotations from Seneca with Aeschylus, *Prometheus Vinctus*, 1, 105: 'the force of necessity is irresistible.
5 'Our deeds determine us as much as we determine our deeds': G. Eliot, *Adam Bede*, chapter 29.
6 Marcuse, *One Dimensional Man*, chapter 1.
7 Seneca, *Nineteenth Letter On Progress*; Lucretius, *De Rerum Natura*; Rousseau, *First and Second Discourse*; Marx, *1844 Manuscripts*, and more recently McCloskey, 1976.
8 Midgley briefly attacks misconceived ways of contrasting innate and cultural. See *Beast and Man*, 1978, pp. 19–24.

CHAPTER III   HARM: OBJECTIVE OR SUBJECTIVE?

1 For example, see Bond, 1983, p. 123.
2 Why is it sometimes thought that death cannot be a harm? The obstacle is that a dead person is not in a state of being harmed or deprived, and this seems to put in jeopardy the claim that the loss of life has a subject. However, this is a problem only if we assume that something can harm us if it causes us to be in a state of deprivation. Death deprives us of all the goods of life; being put in a permanent coma harms a person in much the same way as death does. [This example also illustrates the fact that death need not be a harm, because a person who has been in a permanent irreversible coma loses nothing good by his death.] On death as a harm, see Nagel, 1979, pp. 3–10; Feinberg, 1977, pp. 299–308; and Bond, 1983, p. 128.
3 Nagel, 1979, p. 3.
4 It is more usual to distinguish intrinsic and extrinsic value. I avoid this, the more usual terminology, because it can be confusing. In a sense, harm is intrinsically bad, because it is an intrinsic feature of the concept 'harm' that harm is bad. Nevertheless, harm has secondary negative value. Secondary values include both the instrumentally valuable and constituted values.
5 For discussions of this contrast see Griffin, 1981, section 3, and 1982, section 2; Feinberg, 1977, pp. 302–3 and Sumner, 1981.
6 Nozick, 1974, pp. 42–5. See Griffin, 1981, section 3.
7 It certainly does not rule out *all* versions of the desire theory of harm.

Primarily the desire theory is an answer to question 2 (p. 44) rather than an answer to question 1. Its primary role is to explain why primary goods are good, rather than to say what those primary goods are. So the desire theory can easily accommodate the points made about awareness; it can specify that only certain types of desire count towards well-being and harm, i.e. those which satisfy some awareness condition. See Griffin, 1982, section 4.

8 These points are made forcibly by Sumner, 1981, p. 183. However, Sumner takes them to be arguments against *any* desire theory of harm which is his first mistake (see note 7). His second mistake is to argue for the truth of the mental-state account from the falsehood of the desire account.

9 See Feinberg, 1977, p. 305 and also Nagel, 1979, pp. 4–6.

10 Nagel (1979) accepts posthumous harm for confused reasons, similar to Feinberg's. First, he seems to think that any denial of posthumous harm must entail that secret betrayal is not bad. Secondly, like Feinberg, he suggests that the denial of posthumous harm entails that death cannot be a harm. This is not so, because death deprives us of activities and experiences, but posthumous harm does not. Thirdly, he confuses the propositions 'we must be aware of what harms us', 'we must be aware of the fact that we are harmed', which are both false, with the true proposition 'what we are deprived of when we are harmed are aspects of living which come within the ambit of awareness'. Nagel argues that harm can transcend the bounds of consciousness because it is a deprivation of possibilities. With this I agree, but the point is that the possibilities are possible activities and experiences and that these involve consciousness. Nagel confuses the nature of harm with the nature of what we are deprived of when we are harmed.

11 The informed desire account of well-being is advanced by Frey, 1980, pp. 132–5; Rawls, 1973, pp. 416–24; and Griffin, 1981, pp. 51–62, sections 1–4.

12 Brandt, 1979, p. 250, argues that the informed desire account should be rejected because it cannot rank present and future informed desires. However, Griffin, 1981, section 4 and 1982, section 4, has argued that this problem is not insurmountable.

13 The point is this: the relative value of primary goods is not constituted by the fact that they would be desired or chosen under ideal conditions. This is because the reason why they would be desired is that the subject would appreciate or perceive their relative worth. In other words, the informed desire theory already assumes what it sets out to explain.

14 Frey, 1980, pp. 134–5.

15 Griffin, 1981, section 4.

16 See p. 46.

17 Platts, 1980, pp. 73–84.

18 Moral realism is the view that moral and value predicates are descriptive of reality or that judgments using such predicates present claims which are true or false in virtue of the real world independently of our recognition.

19 This point is made by Norman, 1971, p. 63, who advances an argument similar to Platts', throughout chapter 3 in *Reasons for Action*.

20 See Nagel, 1970, pp. 27–36.

21 The prudential desirability of doing A can be explained with reference to the agent's own desires, but not a desire to do specifically A, because the weak thesis, that Platts should be arguing for, says that a person can have a reason to do A without his desiring to do A.

22 In other words, we can accept that sometimes a person's desire to do A is to be explained with reference to the fact that he believes A to be desirable. In such a case, the subject's desire to do A will not be the reason why A is desirable. Yet, the desirability of A can be explained with reference to the agent's other desires.

23 Peters, 1971, p. 147.

24 See Chapter V, p. 82 and p. 87.

25 By extending this idea, we can regard flourishing as P's life style fitting his nature like a glove and harm as a poor fit between the two.

26 See, for instance. Scanlon, 1975, p. 656.

27 Anscombe, 1976 p. 68.

28 R. Brandt, 1979, p. 26 and pp. 25–35.

29 Kenny, 1975, p. 53.

CHAPTER IV   INTERESTS: THE ROOTS OF DESIRE

1 S. Freud, vol. 14, 1964, p. 111.

2 A point made by Hare, 1972, pp. 55–76. But Hare draws from this the conclusion that anything can be good.

3 See Foot, 1981, pp. 120–3. For a discussion of the differences between Hare and Foot's position see Chapter V. There I argue that a person can desire anything, but that it is not a *real* possibility that anything could be a human interest, and, for this reason, not anything can be good. But, against Foot and in favour of Hare, 1972, I contend that this is because of natural, rather than logical, constraints.

4 Our interests are independent of our beliefs about the desirability and availability of what answers those interests. Suppose, for instance, that many of our desires are motivated by religious interests pertaining to union with God. If this were so, then this would be true of atheists and agnostics as well as theists. But it would be false to say that atheists desired union with God.

5 Scanlon, 1975, pp. 655–69.

6 See, p. 68.

7 See pp. 61–2.

8 Hollis, 1977, p. 3.

9 Morton, 1980, p. 139.

CHAPTER V THE NATURAL LIMITS OF CHOICE

1 Moore, 1956, see pp. 44–5.
2 Warnock, 1978, pp. 28–30.
3 Hare, 1964, pp. 68–9.
4 Hare, 1964, p. 69.
5 Hare, 1971, p. 51 and 'Wrongness and Harm', 1972, pp. 97–8.
6 Hare, 1965, pp. 160–2.
7 Hare, 1965, p. 2.
8 This point is made by Brennan, 1977, p. 35.
9 See also p. 87.
10 C. Taylor, 1973, p. 149.
11 Popper, 1972, p. 342.
12 In a sense, interests are like the practical counterpart of Kant's categories naturalised. They are necessary for deliberation, but not formed by deliberation. They form the framework for our desires, without themselves being desires, as the categories are the framework for judgments without being acts of judgment.
13 J. Griffin discusses need theories of welfare as competitors to informed desire theories. However, he does not make the point that the concept of a need requires a theory of welfare rather than providing one. See Griffin, 1982, section 5. J. Feinberg tries to distinguish between harm and benefit on the ground that harm consists in the frustration of needs and the loss of a benefit does not. See Feinberg, 1973, p. 30.

CHAPTER VI RELATIVITY

1 For a different argument to the same conclusion, see Wollheim, 1975, p. 175.
2 See Chapter III, pp. 43–4.
3 See Chapter III pp. 44–8 and Chapter IV, pp. 73–5.
4 See Chapter III, p. 37.
5 These points are raised in Chapter I pp. 5–61.
6 See Chapter II, pp. 27–8.
7 Feinberg, 1973, p. 30 makes the point that the notion of harm can be explained in two ways. However, the manner in which he distinguishes harm and non-benefit is unsatisfactory. He says that a person is harmed when he is deprived of what he needs, and that a non-benefit does not involve the frustration of needs. This characterisation is unsatisfactory, because we require the notion of harm to explain what a need is, and therefore cannot explain harm in terms of need; see Chapter V, p. 89.
8 See Von Wright, 1968: 'to effect the good of a being adversely is not the same as not to affect it favourably.' A person who falls or is below the norm of well-being is harmed. To lose a benefit causes us to be less well-off, but may not cause us to drop below the norm of well-being, and therefore may not cause us harm. If the norm is set at a high level, so that anything less than flourishing counts as harm, then the formula 'A

needs X to avoid harm' is equivalent to the formula 'A needs X to flourish.'

9 Well-being involves positive states of mind for reasons explained on p. 41, Chapter III.

10 See Griffin, 1982, section 6: 'Does the notion of a "basic need" ever provide a cut-off point, except by fairly arbitrary stipulation?'

11 See Benn and Peters, 1959, pp. 144–6.

12 Benn and Peters, 1959, p. 146.

13 See Wellman, 1982, p. 26.

14 See McCloskey, 1976, p. 5, who cites J. Cronin on today's luxuries becoming conventional necessities tomorrow. McCloskey rejects the type of view put forward by Benn and Peters, but he does not distinguish it from the view being put forward here. See also Feinberg, 1973, p. 112: 'the richer we become, the higher we fix the level at which we are required to distinguish between "necessities" and "luxuries".' Feinberg confuses luxuries and mere benefits, because what he says about necessities and luxuries is true of necessities and benefits.

15 As is claimed by Bond, 1983, p. 135.

16 This type of view is urged by Norman, 1971, chapter 3, and Dearden, 1972, pp. 50–64. I suspect that Benn and Peters, 1959, do confuse the two views discussed here, but can find no evidence for this suspicion.

17 See Chapter III, pp. 49–54 and Chapter V p 82, 87.

18 As is argued in Chapter IV, p. 68, n.3.

19 It is a small step to the view rejected here from the position taken by Philips and Mounce, 1969, pp. 234–9. For instance, Philips and Mounce say: 'human good is not independent of the moral beliefs people hold, but is determined by them' (p. 234). They also say: 'there is no common agreement on what constitutes human good and harm', implying that in principle such agreement may not be possible.

CHAPTER VII   NEEDS AND DESIRES

1 Bay, 1968, p. 241: 'to meet human needs is . . . the ultimate purpose of politics.'

2 The differences between the concepts of 'need' and 'desire' are discussed by White, 1975, pp. 108–16 and by Wollheim, 1975, pp. 174–6.

3 Davidson and Mackie argue for the extensionality of causal relation statements; see Mackie, 1974, pp. 250–68 and Davidson, 1975, pp. 82–94.

4 See especially Fitzgerald, 1977, pp. 195–203; Flew, 1977, pp. 213–22; Minogue, 1963, chapter 4, section one and p. 44.

5 For instance Fitzgerald says: 'It is from its very ambiguity that "need" gains its rhetorical strength', 1977, p. 201.

6 See Chapter VIII, pp. 108–9.

7 Griffin, 1982, section 6, argues that it is incorrect to suggest that needs are the bread of life and desires are mere jam. But Griffin only shows that desired things can be more important than needed things; he does

not show that desires can be better reasons than needs.
8 This is not to say that they will like what they desire.

CHAPTER VIII   IS AND OUGHT

1 See Hudson, 1970, p. 304.
2 Fitzgerald, 1977, pp. vii–xvi and pp. 195–212.
3 For instance, Fitzgerald says: '. . . in terms of the categories of fact and value need is almost pathologically ambiguous. . . . To dismiss ambiguity merely as a fault, however, leaves a lot unsaid' (p. 200). 'In general, however, it would be wrong to say that this use of the word is inconsistent; rather it is consistently ambiguous' (p. 201). 'It is from its very ambiguity that "need" gains its rhetorical strength' (p. 201).
4 Fitzgerald, 1977, p. ix; see also p. 206, where he says of 'need': 'a concept that contains and confuses both elements'.
5 Minogue, 1963, chapter 4, section 1.
6 Maslow, 1959, pp. 123 and 151.
7 Foot, 1981, pp. 110–31, and Warnock, 1967, pp. 55–61.
8 Prescriptivist writers on 'need' include Hudson, 1970, pp. 311–20; Hare, 1972, pp. 92–109; Dearden, 1972, pp. 50–64; Flew, 1977, pp. 213–21; Fitzgerald, 1977, pp. 195–212.
9 Dearden, 1972, pp. 50–64.
10 See Chapter II, pp. 27–8.
11 Hare, 1972, pp. 92–109. 'Wrongness & Harm'.
12 Harman, 1977, pp. 115–24.
13 Hare, 1964, p. 5.
14 For instance, Hare says: 'It is a tautology to say that we cannot sincerely assent to a second person command addressed to ourselves, and at the same time not perform it' (1964, p. 20).
15 Hart, 1961, p. 124.
16 Compare the indexes of Hare, 1964, and 1965, with Hare, 1981.
17 See Hare, 1981, p. 42.
18 Hare, 1981, p. 59.
19 Hare, 1981, p. 59.
20 It is debatable whether Ross actually held this view, and so the title is for convenience.
21 Searle, 1978, pp. 81–91.
22 Searle, 1978, p. 86.
23 Searle, 1978.

CHAPTER IX   MAKING A VIRTUE OF NECESSITY

1 See Chapter I, pp. 18–22.
2 Or more accurately, the antecedent of a necessary condition statement which specifies a fundamental need.
3 As we have seen, this places interesting constraints on the notion of

harm. It is one of the factors which leads us to consider more critically the role of desire in an account of harm and to suggest the notion of an inescapable interest.

4 See pp. 27 and 92.

5 This is not to say that both reasons cannot be overridden by a yet stronger reason.

6 See Warnock, 1967, 'The Object of Morality'.

7 To do so would be to undermine the very point of the evaluation.

BIBLIOGRAPHY

ANSCOMBE, G.E., 1958, 'Modern Moral Philosophy', *Philosophy*, vol. 33, pp. 1–19.

ANSCOMBE, G.E., 1976, *Intention*, Blackwell.

ARONOFF, J., 1967, *Psychological Needs and Cultural Systems*, Van Nostrand.

BARRY, B., 1965, *Political Argument*, Routledge & Kegan Paul.

BAY, C., 1958, *The Structure of Freedom*, Stanford University Press.

BAY, C., 1968, 'Needs, Wants and Political Legitimacy', *Canadian Journal of Political Science*, vol. 1, September 1968, pp. 241–50.

BAY, C., 1977, 'Human Needs and Political Education', in R. Fitzgerald (ed.), *Human Needs and Politics*, Pergamon.

BENN, S. and PETERS, R.S., 1959, *Social Principles and the Democratic State*, Allen & Unwin.

BOND, E.J., 1983, *Reason and Value*, Cambridge University Press.

BRANDT, R., 1979, *A Theory of the Good and the Right*, Clarendon Press.

BRAYBROOKE, D., 1968, 'Let Needs Diminish that Preferences may Prosper', in N. Rescher (ed.), *Studies in Moral Philosophy*, Blackwell, pp. 86–107.

BRENNAN, J., 1977, *The Open Texture of Moral Concepts*, Macmillan.

DAVIDSON, D., 1975, 'Causal Relations' in Sosa (ed.), *Causation and Conditionals*, Oxford University Press, pp. 82–94.

DEARDEN, R., 1972, ' "Needs" in Education' in R. Dearden, P. Hirst and R. Peters (eds.), *Development of Reason*, Routledge & Kegan Paul, pp. 50–64.

FEINBERG, J., 1973, *Social Philosophy*, Prentice-Hall.

FEINBERG, J., 1977, 'Harm and Self-Interest' in P. Hacker and J. Raz (eds.), *Law, Morality and Society*, Clarendon, pp. 285–308.

FITZGERALD, R., 1977, *Human Needs and Politics*, Pergamon.

FLEW, A., 1977, 'Wants or Needs, Choices or Commands?' in R. Fitzgerald (ed.), *Human Needs and Politics*, Pergamon, pp. 213–28.

138

Bibliography

FLEW, A., 1981, *The Politics of Procrustes*, Temple-Smith.

FOOT, P., 1981, *Virtues and Vices*, Blackwell.

FREUD, S., 1964, 'Instincts and their Vicissitudes' in the *Standard Edition of the Psychological Works of S. Freud*, Volume 14, p. 111, International University Press.

FREY, R., 1980, *Interests and Rights*, Clarendon.

FROMM, E., 1967, *Man for Himself*, Routledge & Kegan Paul.

GRIFFIN, J., 1981, 'On Life's Being Valuable', *Dialectics and Humanism*, Vol. 8, no. 2, pp. 51–62.

GRIFFIN, J., 1982, 'Modern Utilitarianism', *Revue Internationale de Philosophie*, no. 131, pp. 331–75.

HARE, R., 1964, *The Language of Morals*, Oxford University Press.

HARE, R., 1965, *Freedom and Reason*, Oxford University Press.

HARE, R., 1971, 'Wanting: Some Pitfalls' in R. Hare (ed.), *Practical Inferences*, Macmillan, pp. 44–59.

HARE, R., 1972, *Essays on the Moral Concepts*, Macmillan.

HARE, R., 1981, *Moral Thinking*, Clarendon.

HARMAN, G., 1977, *The Nature of Morality*, Oxford University Press.

HART, H., 1961, *The Concept of Law*, Clarendon.

HOLLIS, M., 1977, *Models of Man*, Cambridge University Press.

HOTOPF, W., 1964, 'Need in Psychology' in J. Gould and W. Kolb (eds), *Dictionary of Social Sciences*, Tavistock, pp. 462–4.

HUDSON, W., 1970, *Modern Moral Philosophy*, Macmillan.

KAUFMAN, A., 1971, 'Wants, Needs and Liberalism', *Inquiry*, vol. 14, no. 3, pp. 191–212.

KENNY, A., 1963, *Act, Emotion and Will*, Routledge & Kegan Paul.

KENNY, A., 1975, *Will, Freedom and Power*, Blackwell.

KOFFKA, K., 1962, *Principles of Gestalt Psychology*, International Library of Psychology, Philosophy and Scientific Method.

KOMISAR, B., 1961, ' "Need" and the Needs-Curriculum' in B.O. Smith and R. Ennis (eds), *Language and Concepts*, Rand McNally, pp. 24–42.

McCLOSKEY, H., 1976, 'Human Needs, Rights and Political Values', *American Philosophical Quarterly*, vol. 13, no. 1, pp. 1–11.

MACKIE, J., 1974, *The Cement of the Universe*, Clarendon.

MARCUSE, H., 1964, *One Dimensional Man*, Routledge & Kegan Paul.

MASLOW, A., 1954, *Motivational and Personality*, Harper & Row.

MASLOW, A., 1959, *New Knowledge in Human Values*, Harper & Row.

MIDGELY, M., 1978, *Beast and Man*, Harvester.

MILLER, D., 1976, *Social Justice*, Oxford University Press.

MINOGUE, K., 1963, *The Liberal Mind*, Methuen.

MOORE, G.E., 1956, *Principia Ethica*, Cambridge University Press.

MORTON, A., 1980, *Frames of Mind*, Oxford University Press.

MURRAY, H., 1938, *Explorations in Personality*, Oxford University Press.

NAGEL, T., 1970, *The Possibility of Altruism*, Oxford University Press.

NAGEL, T., 1979, 'Death' in *Moral Questions*, Cambridge University Press, pp. 1–11.

NIELSON, K., 1963, 'On Human Needs and Moral Appraisals', *Inquiry*, vol. 6, 1963, pp. 170–83.

Bibliography

NIELSON, K., 1969, 'Morality and Needs' in J. MacIntosh and J. Coval (eds), *The Business of Reason*, Routledge & Kegan Paul, pp. 186–206.

NORMAN, R., 1971, *Reasons for Action*, Blackwell.

NOZICK, R., 1974, *Anarchy, State and Utopia*, Blackwell.

PETERS, R.S., 1960, *The Concept of Motivation*, Routledge & Kegan Paul.

PETERS, R.S., 1971, *Ethics and Education*, Allen & Unwin.

PETERS, R.S. and HIRST, P., 1970, *The Logic of Education*, Routledge & Kegan Paul.

PHILIPS, D. and MOUNCE, 1969, 'On Morality's Having a Point' in W. Hudson (ed.), *The Is-Ought Question*, Macmillan, pp. 228–40.

PLATTS. M., 1979, *Ways of Meaning*, Routledge & Kegan Paul.

PLATTS, M., 1980, 'Morality and the End of Desire' in M. Platts (ed.), *Reference, Truth and Reality*, Routledge & Kegan Paul.

POPPER, K., 1972, *Objective Knowledge*, Oxford University Press.

RAWLS, J., 1973, *A Theory of Justice*, Oxford University Press.

RICHARDS, D., 1970, *A Theory of Reasons for Action*, Oxford University Press.

ROSEN, F., 1977, 'Basic Needs and Justice', *Mind*.

SCANLON, T., 1975, 'Preference and Urgency' in *Journal of Philosophy*, no. 72, pp. 655–69.

SEARLE, J., 1978, 'Prima Facie Obligations' in Raz (ed.), *Practical Reasoning*, Oxford University Press, pp. 81–91.

SOPER, K., 1981, *On Human Needs*, Harvester.

SPARSHOTT, F., 1958, *An Inquiry into Goodness*, Toronto University Press.

SPRINGBORG, P., 1981, *The Problem of Human Needs and the Critique of Civilisation*, Allen & Unwin.

SUMNER, L., 1981, *Abortion and Moral Theory*, Princeton University Press.

TAYLOR, C., 1973, 'Neutrality and Political Science' in Ryan (ed.), *The Philosophy of Social Explanation*, Oxford University Press, pp. 139–70.

TAYLOR, P., 1959, ' "Need"-Statements', *Analysis*, vol. 19, no. 5, pp. 106–11.

WARNOCK, G., 1967, *Contemporary Moral Philosophy*, Macmillan.

WARNOCK, G., 1978, 'On Choosing Values', *The Mid-West Studies in Philosophy*, vol. III.

WELLMAN, C., 1982, *Welfare Rights*, Rowman & Littlefield.

WHITE, A., 1975, *Modal Thinking*, Blackwell.

WIGGINS, D., 1976, 'Truth, Invention and the Meaning of Life', *Proceedings of the British Academy*, vol. 62, pp. 331–78.

WILLIAMS, B., 1981, *Moral Luck*, Cambridge University Press.

WOLLHEIM, R., 1975, 'Needs, Desires and Moral Turpitude', *Nature and Conduct*, Royal Institute of Philosophy Lectures, Volume VIII, Macmillan, pp. 162–79.

WRIGHT, P. and TAYLOR, A., 1972, *Introducing Psychology*, Penguin.

WRIGHT, V., 1968, *The Varieties of Goodness*, Routledge & Kegan Paul.

INDEX